The Christian Camp Leader

Jim Badke

With a solid spiritual foundation and a rich understanding of both campers and young adult camp leaders, Jim gives a realistic picture of camp life, with practical guidance and a godly perspective.

– Dan Everest, Christian Camp & Conference Association

Jim is a consummate camp leader who packs a lifetime of experience and a wealth of wisdom in these pages. This book is the one essential tool in any camp leader's survival kit.

– Mark Buchanan, Ambrose Seminary

---

campleader.ca

Purchase information, bulk sales, articles, author contact and more.

How do you equip young leaders for the daunting task of accompanying a herd of campers through an intensely relational week of camp programming? This little volume covers it all. Next to a book on how to rub sticks together to start a fire in the rain, this will be the most valuable book in your camp ministry library.

– Marv Penner, Youth Specialties Canada

Jim Badke has done it again. He has created another indispensable resource by capturing the essence of why and how ministry takes place at camp. The Christian Camp Leader is well written, accessible and concise, showing rookies - and reminding veterans - what camp ministry is all about.

– Bill McCaskell, One Hope Canada

We have used Jim's books for staff training at all levels, including our counselor in training program, and could not have asked for a better resource. His latest edition is simple, straightforward and applicable for all of our summer staff.

– Andrea Jackson, Program Director, Stillwood Camp

A concise, easily read book to equip young workers with the core skills, attitudes and passion they will need to be outstanding Christian camp leaders. In my 32 years of experience of working at camps this is the best resource I have found to prepare new staff to care for campers.

– Randy Carter, Camp Speaker, Straight Talk Ministries

Puts the focus where it's needed: on the campers and the personal spiritual preparedness of the leader they look up to.

– Les Klassen, Campfire Ministries

This book focuses its reader on Christ and God's word, while driving home the importance of discipleship as a foundation in camping ministry. A must use resource for equipping camp ministry leaders to succeed!

– Nancy Paschke, Leadership Director, Camp Nutimik

--- More reviews at Amazon.com ---

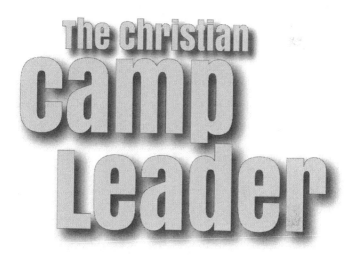

Jim Badke Author of
The Christian Camp Counselor

THE CHRISTIAN CAMP LEADER by Jim Badke
Copyright ©2013 James Badke - Second Revision, 2018

campleader.ca • jimbadke@gmail.com

Original Cover Design by davej at ArtDesignLife.com
Editing by Charis St. Pierre
Cover Photos: Karen Ann Kane, Camp Imadene - imadene.com

Also available in Kindle eBook and Audible audiobook formats from amazon.com, which can be read or heard on any device with the Kindle or Audible app.

Is your organization interested in translating this book? Please contact jimbadke@gmail.com.

Jim Badke is the author of *The Christian Camp Counselor*, 1998. *The Christian Camp Leader* is a new book, though brief portions were freely adapted from his former book, without reference. *The Christian Camp Counselor* is still available from:

- English: Camp Qwanoes, qwanoes.ca
- Portuguese: CCI Brasil, cci.org.br/loja/
- Spanish: Juventud Para Cristo, co.yfci.org

CONTENTS

You Were Made For This!

In the beginning, God created. This is a very good place to start.

People have different ideas about how the world came to be. I am pretty sure none of us knows what we are talking about and when we get to heaven we are all in for a big surprise.

I just believe what God says: that he made it all. And by believing this, I understand a number of concepts that are critical for anyone (like you) who has the desire in their heart to serve at a Christian camp. The apostle Paul tells us "we are God's handiwork, created in Christ Jesus to do good works, which God prepared in advance for us to do" (Eph 2:10). So I am an intentional creation. I am not just the result of a number of random pieces coming together after eons of tries. I was made and formed, shaped and sculpted. God calls me his workmanship, his craftsmanship, his masterpiece. What's more, he has specific things in mind for me to do in this world. This means I was designed, planned, calculated! All the parts of me—the bits I like and the ones I don't—form the person who can accomplish the things God has in mind for me to do.

There's more: God prepared in advance everything he designed me to do. It is already set up. It will often be hard to understand how it all fits together, but the picture was formed before I was born and every day he hands me more pieces of the puzzle. I can be confident in how God has designed me and arranged my story. Even when I mess up, God takes action to bring my mistakes back into line with his purpose. His grace is like the stream on the beach my boys used to try to dam up. It always found another way to do the thing it was designed to do.

If God is calling you to serve at a Christian camp this summer, you can be confident of two things:

You were made for this.

And God has already gone ahead and prepared the way for you to do it.

Your camp may have asked you to read this book before you arrive, so I have tried to make your reading experience as painless and interesting as possible. The first section is about personal preparation for entering the camp environment, and my hope is you will love Jesus all the more as you read. The second part explains how to manage your role well and not be toast at the end of it. My prayer is your experience will be one of the best memories of your entire life, as you partner with God in the incredible setting of camp ministry.

PART ONE: I WANT TO BECOME A CAMP LEADER

1. Be a Disciple

If you decided to get a job at a shoe factory this summer instead of serving at camp, it would be important to have an understanding of your end product. You would need to know what a shoe is and the process for making one. So what is the end product of a Christian camp?

Jesus told us: "Therefore go and **make disciples** of all nations, baptizing them in the name of the Father and of the Son and of the Holy Spirit, and teaching them to obey everything I have commanded you. And surely I am with you always, to the very end of the age" (Matt 28:19-20). At a Christian camp, *disciples* are what we do.

What is a disciple? In Jesus' day, a disciple was someone who had been invited to follow a rabbi or teacher, which meant he would leave the life he was leading and go wherever his rabbi went, with the intention of becoming like the rabbi and joining him in his work. In the same way, Jesus tells us that as we go, we are to produce people who will follow him, become like him and do what he is doing in the world.

How do people become disciples of Jesus? If it were simply a matter of each person deciding to become one, Jesus would not have told us to go and "make disciples." In the original language these two words are actually one verb, so perhaps a closer translation might be, "Go and *disciplize* all nations." If that is too technical for you, try this:

Disciples produce disciples.

This is no shoe factory; it is more like a sci-fi flick where robots replicate themselves. Wherever there are disciples, you should expect more to appear over time. If you want to "make disciples" at camp as Jesus commanded us, you need to be one yourself. The essence of discipleship is to say to someone, "Follow my example, as I follow the example of Christ" (1 Cor 11:1).

Whew! If that makes you feel like closing this book and calling up the camp director to tell him you are not coming, I understand. But give me a chance before you do.

When Jesus called people to follow him—that is, become his disciples—the invitation was two-sided: it was a call to turn away from one thing in order to pursue another. Jesus met a rich young guy who seemed to be doing all the right things. Jesus looked at him and loved him and told him he was missing something. Sell everything, he said, give it all away and then come follow me (Mark 10:17-21). Wow.

1. BE A DISCIPLE

Leave everything and follow!

Maybe you grew up in the church, asked Jesus into your heart at a young age and did everything expected of you all your life. But you know something is missing. I want you to hear this: Jesus loves you. You have heard this before, but it is true. Maybe he is calling you today to leave something (I don't know what) so you can follow him. Be his disciple. Become like him and join him in his work.

Notice what I am doing here: As a disciple of Jesus, I am *disciplizing* you. Through my words, I am pointing you to Jesus, with the hope that God the Father will extend his grace to you and his Holy Spirit will stir in your heart. I hope as a result you will decide (or decide again) to leave everything and follow Jesus. In other words, you will turn away from all that is good about you and all that is not, and put your trust in Jesus. You will become his disciple.

Please don't be offended like the rich young man. I respect your Christian experience or wherever you are coming from. But I don't know who is reading this, and there is no point going any further in this book until we deal with the question: Are you a disciple of Jesus? If not, today is the day. And if today is not the day, please go ahead and make the phone call to the camp director.

Maybe you are a disciple but you are feeling defeated. It doesn't take drug addiction or sleeping around. One of Satan's best (or worst) strategies is to lead us down a path of small defeats—in our devotions, our prayer life, our witnessing, maybe a few habits like porn or overindulgence, a problem with gossip, a few people we have never forgiven.

Before we know it we are trapped in a cycle of inconsistency and guilt. I've been there before, and I know: it is like being aware you are drowning, and if you could just get your head above water for a minute you would do something about it. Again, today is the day. Please don't wait until the week before you go to camp.

When you put your faith in Jesus, all of these sins are forgiven, removed from you as far as the east is from the west. You trust that Jesus took upon himself the consequences of your sin as he hung on a cross. You are forgiven for the past, the present and the future, and you are made right with God. Your faith in Christ is an act of turning away from all you are and turning to God; or using the language of discipleship, you leave everything to follow Jesus. Your faith is not only in what he did for you but in Jesus himself. In his person, his work, his character, his holiness, his righteousness, his purity, his love. This faith demands a change of thinking; for example, in order to believe in Jesus there are many things in which you have to stop believing. It is a change of loyalties: from building your own kingdom to building his.

Do you remember Indiana Jones stepping off a ledge onto a rock bridge he couldn't see? As a disciple of Jesus, you step out of one life to pursue another, placing all your weight on him alone. It is like letting go of one rope in the challenge course so you can reach the next. The transformation of your value system alone may be very confusing to those who knew you before; "They are surprised that you do not join them in their reckless, wild living, and they heap abuse on you" (1 Peter 4:4). You start to make decisions from a whole new set of principles: love your enemies, do good to people who try to use you.

You find yourself giving up your independence and your attempts at self-sufficiency, and you let him provide for you on this journey of following him. You take Jesus at his word when he said, "You may ask me for anything in my name, and I will do it" (John 14:14). You begin to change inside so more and more you love what he loves and hate what he hates. You feel his compassion, his heartbreak, his indignation, his anger. You think his thoughts after him. His character appears on you, like fruit growing on a tree. Love, joy, peace, patience, kindness, goodness, faithfulness, gentleness, self-control (Gal 5:22-23). You see your sin the way he sees it, not dressed up and Photoshopped the way the world does. Other people come to understand God more clearly just by being with you.

It is utter abandon.

But rather than lose your identity, you are turning into the person you truly were meant to be. When you leave all to follow Jesus, you start a journey of becoming more you than you have ever been in all your years; as unique as a thumbprint yet more and more like the One you are following.

I don't want you to arrive at camp, unpack your bags and discover to your shock and amazement that things you thought you left at home came with you. I'm not talking Archie comics; I mean the ragged baggage of your heart and lifestyle: bitterness and blame; lust and envy; doubt and rebellion; addictions and dependencies; prejudice or feelings of worthlessness; harmful coping mechanisms; pride and arrogance; shame and despair.

I call on you to leave everything and follow Jesus.

"But I am already a Christian," you say! Is the word "Christian" something by which the world describes you, or are you someone who describes who "Christ" is to the world? Disciples represent their master. Becoming a leader in a camp setting is an incredible opportunity to show kids, youth and adults who Jesus is, by your faith expressed in everything you do with them.

My first camp cabin leader was a guy named Rob. I would have done anything for the guy, he was that cool. When we were around Rob, we all felt important, like what we cared about actually mattered because when we talked he paid attention to us instead of the cute lifeguards. When he spoke about Jesus, Rob was talking about a guy he knew personally; his life showed us who Jesus was. He sent me a letter in the mail—twice—and I carried them in my Bible for several years. I decided in the course of one week I wanted to be just like Rob.

Follow Jesus, and people around you will begin to follow him as they follow you. Take that idea to camp this summer and the effect will be amazing, as you and your campers do sleepovers every night, go out for every meal and in one week play more games and enjoy more recreation than you have in the whole past year. The crazy wonderfulness of camp is an ideal environment for discipleship.

As a follower of Jesus who wants to become a

leader, you need to understand his style of leadership. One day, two of his disciples tried to pull a fast one on their buddies by asking Jesus to make them next-in-command in his kingdom. As word got out about this, Jesus stopped the impending fight by telling his ragamuffins that leadership in his kingdom would be different from the bullying they were used to. "Instead, whoever wants to be great among you must be your servant, and whoever wants to be first must be slave of all. For even the Son of Man did not come to be served, but to serve, and to give his life as a ransom for many" (Mark 10:43-45). Jesus came to take over the world, and servanthood was his method.

Well, how would that work? Who is going to listen to a servant?

Did you ever have a teacher in school you couldn't stand? How well did you do in their class? Think of leaders who showed they cared and whom you wanted to please. Do you remember thinking how you wanted to be just like them? Jesus is the teacher we want to work for; the hero we want to be like. In everything he did with his disciples, Jesus was saying, "This is the kind of leader I want you to be."

Following Jesus' style of servant-leadership will work effectively for you as a camp leader. Imagine this: It must be 2:00 AM when you wake to hear a few sniffles and a quiet sob from a bunk in the corner of the cabin. Great—a homesick camper, or maybe even a wet sleeping bag. It would be so easy to roll over and pretend you didn't hear it; no one will ever know. But instead, you get up and deal gently and quietly with the camper, and it is an hour later when your head hits the pillow again.

What happened in your cabin is not just about camper rest or hygiene. In a camper's bad moment, intensified by the angst of being eight years old, you were there. Jesus was there, in your attention and whispered assurances. That camper will be different tomorrow, with a heart open to hear what you have to say and eyes attentive to the way you do things. You have built trust, and it will make a difference.

Try this next time you are in a crowd that you know fairly well, like a class at school or your church: See if there is someone there that you have never noticed before. Chances are, someone has never come within your radar. Jesus always seemed to find those ones in the crowd, the unnoticed minority. You will have kids who are quiet or unattractive or unpleasant or who have "high maintenance" written all over them. Jesus in you would say, "It is not the healthy who need a doctor, but the sick" (Matt 9:12). Let the unloved become high priority to you like they are to him, and they will respond in ways the cool kids will not.

I think I should warn you: your influence can also go the other way. Jesus' warning was brutal: "If anyone causes one of these little ones—those who believe in me—to stumble, it would be better for them to have a large millstone hung around their neck and to be drowned in the depths of the sea" (Matt 18:6). Please take your leadership very seriously, because God does. Your daily decisions will affect not only you; they have the power to do great good or great harm to your campers.

You will need to pray hard for love and wisdom, as Paul prayed for his church, "that your love may

2. Connect with God

Your connection with God is vitally important to your spiritual health and development. Maybe that sounds like something your dentist always tells you about flossing, but it is true. Jesus put it this way: "I am the vine; you are the branches. If you remain in me and I in you, you will bear much fruit; apart from me you can do nothing" (John 15:5).

Connected, the life of Jesus flows through his followers so they have everything they need to become like him and join him in his work. You will need that at camp this summer, sometimes desperately. Disconnected, you will find yourself going through the motions but producing nothing, like a printer that has run out of ink.

Ever feel that way?

We are connected with God through our faith in Jesus. Have you ever wondered about the phrase we tack onto the end of most prayers: "In Jesus' name, amen"? Imagine for a moment what you really need is a brand new Lamborghini, but you are about a million dollars short of getting one. You go to the bank, ask for a loan, and they begin to laugh politely. But then you show them your ID—"Bill Gates, Jr."—and mention your dad will be by shortly to co-sign the loan. Suddenly their attitude changes, and soon you are behind the wheel of a very nice car. Dad's name on the bottom line made all the difference (don't ask why Dad doesn't just give you the money – it messes up my analogy).

In Jesus' name, we access the power and authority of God. When we pray and speak and act in his name, Jesus signs the bottom line. Of course, he will never sign something that doesn't line up with the will of God; what we ask for must represent him well. Jesus said, "All authority in heaven and earth has been given me" (Matt 28:18), and as we speak and act in his name we gain access to this awesome power, through our faith in him and his grace toward us. We are highly privileged people.

Having access to God's power through Jesus is one thing—drawing on it is another. When you are not employing the power of God through faith in Jesus, your enemy the devil will be quite content to let you mess things up on your own. There are several "spiritual disciplines" you can put into practice which are part of the training and lifestyle of a disciple of Jesus, and by which you access the power and authority of God:

Worship is offering yourself to God as a sacrifice made acceptable to him through Jesus. Gratitude, praise and adoration are our response to the love he has shown us. When we worship God we begin to see things from his perspective: gratefulness reminds us of the good God has given us; honoring him makes us consider who he is; praise enumerates his good works in the world; wonder marvels at his power and character. Worship produces confidence in the God we serve.

Prayer is an expression of your faith in God and your desire to see things happen, so when you pray God goes to work. He spoke and the world was created; he also invites you to speak things into being that otherwise would never be, praying in Jesus' name. A peculiar tone has crept into the prayers of the Western church, represented by the word "just." It is like we don't want to bother God too much: "Just give me strength to manage this tough cabin." "God, just bless this chapel time and meet with us." It sounds spiritual, but I challenge you to drop the word and its tone from your prayer vocabulary. Jesus invites us to pray with "shameless audacity" (Luke 11:8), boldly daring to ask God for what only God can do. That way, his answers to our specific requests bring him all the credit he deserves.

Confession is seeing our sin the way Jesus sees it. As a result, we turn away from our sin and trust in him again. Jesus compares confession to getting our feet washed—we have had the "bath" of salvation but tend to get our feet dirty as we walk around in the world (John 13:10). Rather than pretend our feet smell fine, "if we confess our sins, he is faithful and just and will forgive us our sins and purify us from all unrighteousness" (1 John 1:9). Like David, ask God to search your heart and your anxious thoughts, and see if there is any offensive way in you (Ps 139:23-24). God will show you the sin needing confession. Know that because of his great love for you and your faith in Jesus, he removes your sin as far from you as the east is from the west (Ps 103:11-12).

Bible study goes beyond just reading the word of God; it is digging deeper with the intention of understanding what it says and means, and deciding what to do about it. The Holy Spirit draws our attention to concepts we need to notice, both for our sake and so we can teach them to others. He enables us to understand the central truth of the passage we are reading, the Big Idea we most need to know. Then he stirs in our hearts to prompt the changes needed so we will be doers of his word and not hearers only (James 1:22-25). This process is essential to your training as a disciple. Consider it not a dull duty, but a daily journey in which you will be taught, rebuked, corrected and trained in righteousness, so you will be thoroughly equipped for every good work (2 Tim 3:16-17).

Meditation follows your intent reading of the word of God. Many people think meditation requires emptying your mind, but one of the meanings of the word is to "ruminate," which is more like the biblical concept. Just like a cow regurgitates its food during the day and chews it again (sorry, but it's true), you can recall and re-digest his word and allow the Spirit to influence your thoughts and actions. Meditation leads to application; as you take moments throughout the day to ponder God's word, it shapes your attitudes and lifestyle.

Solitude was the regular practice of Jesus, who often withdrew to quiet, undisturbed places to hear from God and make important decisions or stand against temptation. We seem to be afraid of silence. We get in the car and turn on the iPod; the TV is on when no one is even watching it; a pause in a conversation makes us feel awkward and embarrassed. Perhaps the distractions in our lives are more intentional than we care to admit. Could we be afraid that in a moment of silence, the big picture may cast doubt on the validity of our way of life? Will those quiet moments raise questions we don't want to answer? He invites us to "be still [literally, *stop!* or *cease striving*], and know that I am God" (Ps 46:10).

Stewardship is managing time and resources the way Jesus intends them to be used and prompting others in the world to do the same. It starts with an understanding that everything we have is from God and we are merely managers of it, and therefore we are expected to use what we have to represent well our Master's name and his best interests. We don't have time to waste, but neither should we cram our days with exhausting activity. More than anyone on earth, believers should be the ones to use natural resources carefully and manage our waste responsibly. Ethical sourcing and fair trade should matter to us, so as much as possible, our use of resources doesn't exploit others. Make it your goal to give enough of your resources away that faith in God is required to make it from month to month. Simplicity, not extravagance, marks the lifestyle of disciples of Jesus who are acting as faithful managers of their Father's business.

Speaking and serving are also forms of stewardship. "Each of you should use whatever gift you have received to serve others, as faithful stewards of God's grace in its various forms. If anyone speaks, they should do it as one who speaks the very words of God. If anyone serves, they should do so with the strength God provides, so that in all things God may be praised through Jesus Christ" (1 Peter 4:11). Spiritual gifts are abilities above and beyond natural talents that the Holy Spirit distributes to all believers in Jesus to contribute to the work of the church. As we deploy these supernatural abilities, we become channels of the grace of God to those around us. When God prompts you to serve, obedience will soon show you which spiritual gifts you have been given.

Your **testimony** is where Jesus' story and your story collided—and everything changed for you. Take every opportunity to tell your story. There is no better way to communicate the Gospel to your campers than through the narrative of you and Jesus. Not only will they come to understand and appreciate you better; they will hear an example of how to come to faith in Christ. God will give you the words, and his Spirit will draw people to himself. Hearing one another's story can also deepen the relationships in your cabin, creating an atmosphere of transparency and trust. Give campers an opportunity to respond to one another's story with questions, encouragement and challenge.

Submission is victory in the daily struggle between our rebellious self and the Spirit of God in us. Occasionally it is good to set aside an intentional period of submission to God, in the form of fasting from food or giving up something important to us for a time. Jesus said that when a branch is fruitful, it should be pruned so that it can become even more fruitful. If God is calling you to submit to him in the use of your time and energy, or to give up to him an activity or relationship, understand it is for your spiritual health. Balance is needed—the Bible says harsh treatment of the body is unnecessary and ineffective (Col 2:23)—so periods of fasting should be intentional, beneficial and temporary.

Receiving **guidance** from God comes more easily when we daily practice submission to him. What is his will for you? Most of our decisions can be informed by the values and principles in God's word, which is our main source of wisdom for knowing his will. Occasionally we need to choose between options that all seem good, and then a more specific form of guidance is needed. Rather than push us one way or another through circumstances, God desires hearts that are open to his coaching and instruction, as he told David: "I will instruct you and teach you in the way you should go; I will counsel you with my loving eye on you. Do not be like the horse or the mule, which have no understanding but must be controlled by bit and bridle or they will not come to you" (Ps 32:8-9). God gives wisdom generously to those who ask without doubting him (James 1:5-8). There are times when God will use extraordinary means of communicating what he wants us to do, but don't expect angels or handwriting on the wall very often.

Endurance is given to us as we maintain our trust in Jesus, particularly in challenging times. Even a week of camp can be exhausting to its leaders, and some of you will be serving all summer. What will keep you going? I trust your supervisors will take good care of you and you will be wise in your choices, but it may not be enough. Here is a promise for you: "Even youths shall faint and be weary, and young men shall fall exhausted, but they who wait for the Lord shall renew their strength; they shall run and not be weary, they shall walk and not faint" (Isa 40:30-31, ESV). To wait on God is to keep looking to him with expectation, anticipating what he is about to do. That kind of watching in faith will see you through a lifetime of following him.

Unlike physical training you may have done, spiritual training will exercise your faith in Jesus. But also like any other discipline, it won't happen by sitting on a couch in front of sitcoms with a big bowl of popcorn. This is faith working itself out in action! "Train yourself to be godly. For physical training is of some value, but godliness has value for all things, holding promise for both the present life and the life to come" (1 Tim 4:7-8). Just as you would not run a marathon without an extended period of training, don't expect to do very well if you neglect your spiritual training right up until the time you serve at camp! Reboot your spiritual fitness program now.

Think about this:
- What spiritual disciplines do you have in place already, and which ones will you begin to implement today?

3. Enter the Camp Community

Camp is God's idea. Throughout history, he often called people away from their homes to a specific place and time of encounter and response. In a very large world, God set Adam and Eve in one garden where he walked with them in the cool of the day (Gen 2-3). Abraham became a "friend of God" through close meetings face to face with his Maker in the wilderness (Gen 15). The Israelites were commanded to remember their ancestors' journey through the desert by living in tents for one week a year (Lev 23:41-43). God's people went to camp every summer!

Three times in the Bible we find that God talks of "setting his dwelling"—literally, his "tent"—among his people: in the desert in Sinai (Lev 26:11-12), in the person of Jesus (John 1:14) and in heaven (Rev 21:3). He loves to camp with his people, and will do so forever! Through God's idea that we call "camp," he removes us from our usual setting, relieves us from the usual pressures of everyday life, isolates us from the distractions and temptations of the world, provides optimum conditions for crisis and change, confronts us with our own condition and our need for him, spends focused time with us, teaches us life-altering lessons and finds response, accomplishes something extraordinary that otherwise would not have occurred, sends us back into the world with new understanding and perspective, and causes us to long for the permanent community of heaven.

Today's Christian camp is one of those temporary spiritual environments where people make their most profound and life-changing decisions about faith in the Lord Jesus Christ and commit to following him. The institution of Christian camping emerged from two heritages: in the nineteenth century, secular schools or clubs established camps to pass down outdoor skills to younger generations; about the same time, evangelistic tent meetings drew rural families together to hear from God and enjoy fellowship. The merging of these traditions still lingers in our archery ranges, chapels and altar calls.

Will camp always look as it does today? When God uses a method of ministry to achieve his purposes, we may get so excited about the results we act as if it was the method—rather than God—that was so effective. We expect great spiritual decisions and life changes to happen among campers year after year, and end up puzzled when our methods no longer appear to be working. It may be instead that God is at work in new ways and is no longer using our particular model of "camp." Christian camping needs to stay humble and flexible to the movement of God if it is to progress.

Who are the people that serve as leaders at camp?

Camp ministry is not for everyone. As we have already discussed, leaders at a Christian camp need to be disciples of Jesus so they can make other disciples, but not every disciple is called to camp ministry. Watching many staff arrive at camp every summer has given me a feel for the kind of person who fits in well there, whatever specific role they may have.

Camp people actually enjoy spending time with children and youth—you see them seeking out kids in a crowd more often than hanging back and chatting with their peers. They have an energy and enthusiasm that—whether loud or quiet—draws kids along with them. They find themselves genuinely caring for people they barely know, and look for ways to be kind and thoughtful toward them. The shyest or most rebellious youth want to talk with them. They are the kind of people you hope your own kids will become one day; you don't have to fear for the example they are setting, even when they are acting outrageously.

Although helpful, it is not essential to have a history of attending and serving at camps; newbies sometimes bring freshness to an overworked program. If you are transferring in from another camp, watch first and let humility curb your inclination to tell people how it was done at your last camp. Great camp staff are flexible to last-minute changes and are willing to put up with some inconvenience for a good cause. They should be emotionally stable, since fatigue will magnify conditions such as depression or low self-esteem.

Getting into good physical shape before camp is a very good idea. Having said that, people with physical and mental challenges can perform roles at camp that cannot be as adequately filled by anyone else, full as they are with the grace and graciousness of God.

Camps love innovators who can work within the purpose and direction of the ministry; their creativity keeps kids coming back for more, year after year. We want people who are approachable and welcoming, whose confidence makes kids feel secure and who are not hesitant to offer leadership. Camp is a great place to develop these traits; if you are not there yet, consider going to camp anyway and assisting a more experienced leader. Watch carefully those who are able to teach and coach kids into new understanding and ability—by their fruit you will know them. I love the composure of staff who are quick to listen and slow to speak, who know that what kids want most is to be heard and understood.

Hopefully, these are the qualifications your camp saw in you when they decided to accept you on staff this summer. Now that you have decided to respond to the camp's invitation, what do you need to do to get ready for the incredible adventure ahead of you?

If you have considered carefully the things we have already discussed, you are most of the way there. The preparation of your heart is far more critical than buying the right board shorts or sunscreen. Assuming this, here are some of the more hands-on things to consider.

What are the camp's expectations of you? Smaller camps are often staffed by the same people year after year who know just what to expect; if you are not one of them, you may have to ask some questions to get an idea of what they want you to do and what is in store for you. Many camps will send you helpful information, including training materials, a job description and a staff manual. Read them! Imagine you went into a blind person's house when he wasn't there and moved around all the furniture. What a mean thing to do! The poor guy would stumble over everything because it wasn't where he expected it. You are about to enter a community where many expectations and boundaries may be in places unfamiliar to you, and you don't want to walk in there blind. Please avoid tripping—read the materials that are sent to you.

You will also do your camp a favor by communicating well with them, returning their calls and messages promptly. Do you have special dietary needs or a wedding you need to attend in the middle of summer? Please don't wait until you get to camp to let them know. Have they sent you forms to fill out? It is better to complete them now, rather than wait to arrive at camp and discover you don't have the information with you, or the criminal record check was due a month ago.

Most camps offer training before the busy summer season begins. You may be reading this book as part of that training—well done! Keep on reading! If you can, take every opportunity to participate in weekend workshops or online sessions, both for the wisdom you will receive and the connections you will make with other staff. If you are new to the world of camp, consider volunteering for a weekend retreat before attempting a whole week in the summer, and it is wise to try a week of summer camp before applying to serve for a whole season.

What should you bring with you to camp? I am not going to tell you how much underwear to bring (okay, I will: bring lots!), but here are some of the other essentials you might not think of as you pack:

A good **LED flashlight** or headlamp and extra batteries are a must for most camps, for night games and 2:00 AM trips with a camper to the distant washroom. If the cabins at your camp are without electricity, bring a good LED lantern. Unless someone plays the bagpipes each morning at your camp, you will also need a battery-powered **alarm clock** to wake up you and your campers in the morning. You may find the early hours are the only time for your own Bible reading and prayer.

If you are not sure what **clothing and footwear** to bring to your camp, ask some camp-experienced people. Will sandals be enough, or will your position require close-toed shoes? What is considered modest in swimwear, and do people bring a wetsuit? Will there be any occasions when staff are expected to dress up or to get filthy dirty? Better to ask than wish all week you had brought the right stuff.

In addition to your own Bible, bring a **Bible suitable to the age group** you are leading. It is the shepherd's job to place the feed where the sheep can reach it. For example, Churchsource.com offers the NIrV Pathlight Camper's Bible; the NIrV is like the popular NIV version but at a grade three reading level. Of course, you may have a variety of versions at your fingertips with Bible apps (see bible.com or biblegateway.com), but is the camp okay with you using a cell phone or iPad during your week at camp? Have a paper copy with you as well, and if you bring a study Bible you can access answers to many of the tough questions campers will ask. You may also want to bring a journal to record your experience and to model journaling to your campers. This means you will need **pens** (I am convinced that camp eats pens), so while you are at it throw in some **colored markers and paper** for rainy days and notes to campers.

If you are expected to lead cabin Bible discussions (more on this later), check a Christian bookstore for **resources** appropriate to the age of your campers. As well, ask some experienced camp leaders for their favorite Bible discussion ideas and bring these with you to adapt to your campers' needs. While you are at the bookstore, see if they have any books that offer answers to typical questions campers might ask.

Consider what you can bring to give your cabin group a **sense of identity** and the **feeling of home**. I have seen leaders bring a crazy hat to help campers find them in a crowd, or something they can all wear or a homemade flag to fly from the cabin roof. A large blanket creates a great space for cabin discussions on the floor or grass. Sometimes it is not until you bring out your stuffed animal that campers will sheepishly pull theirs out of the suitcase, providing a sense of security. Have enough of your stuff in the cabin that campers feel it is your home and they are living there with you. Most camps expect you to bring your own **bedding**, and you should have enough clothes and towels that you can get through a week without doing laundry. Bring items that will make life in your cabin comfortable, but be ready to share any and all "luxuries" with your campers! Avoid bringing things that are precious to you; if you would rather die than lose it, leave it at home.

As your time at camp draws near, do some serious heart-searching. Are there any personal issues standing between you and God, or you and another person? What is your motive for coming to camp as a leader? Are you doing it to satisfy your own thirst for fun and adventure and travel? Is it for approval from God, or maybe from people? Or to meet some special guy or girl? Are you seeking revenge from back when you were a camper? Motive matters to God. My prayer is that your decision to go to camp is driven first by a tenacious love for God and second by a compelling love for children and youth.

Think about this:
- What are you feeling really good about for the summer?
- What do you need to work on in preparation for your summer role?

I invite you to pray this biblical prayer for wisdom:

"Lord my God, now you have made me, your servant, a cabin leader at camp. But I'm just a kid myself; I don't know how to do what must be done. I, your servant, am here among your chosen campers, and there seems to be too many to count. I ask you to give me a heart that understands, so I can lead my campers in the right way and will know the difference between right and wrong. Otherwise, it is impossible to lead this great cabin of yours" (1 Kings 3:7-9, with apologies to King Solomon).

4. Provide Leadership

If you were a guest in the camp community, you would be welcomed just as you are. But as a leader, preparation and a higher level of spiritual maturity and responsibility are expected. Arrive ready to serve and contribute! In turn, you should expect the camp's leadership staff to seek to look after your needs. Camps vary in their attitude and attention toward their staff; hopefully, your camp leadership invests in their staff, knowing that if they take great care of their leaders, the leaders will take great care of the campers. The old saying, "Camp is for the campers" has some merit but misses the reality that the people who are most profoundly transformed by the camp experience are the staff.

Just the same, you will be expected to take a great deal of responsibility for yourself at camp. When you applied to camp, they asked your references questions such as: Is he punctual? How does she handle conflict? Is he self-motivated? Does she follow through with tasks? These are the qualities the camp assumes their staff have as they plan a busy summer schedule. The camp also has policies that are there for your protection; if you choose to ignore the rules at the waterfront or some other activity, you remove yourself from their liability coverage and become personally liable for your actions, a risk you cannot afford. You will also need to pace yourself. Camp is fun—you won't want to miss a thing and in all the excitement you might be tempted to give it everything you've got all the time. Pacing yourself is an attitude that says I will not allow what is urgent to pilfer what is important, or what is exciting to burglarize what is essential.

As well as carrying your own load, you will need to work together with the rest of the staff team. Camp is no place for solo efforts. The cabin leader who tries to be exclusive with his group usually creates more work and frustration for everyone else. But a community of staff who watch out for one another creates a caring environment for campers and reduces the load for everyone. Encourage your fellow staff. Ask them regularly how they are doing and how to pray for them. Jesus prayed for unity among his followers so the world would believe in him (John 17:20-21). As the world arrives at camp, a cooperative attitude among staff will be one of the first things they notice.

I hope you get to serve with a great staff team this summer, but you need to realize that "making disciples" is a supernatural work of God that is beyond the capacity of all of you combined. Paul described his ministry in agricultural terms: "I planted the seed, Apollos watered it, but God has been making it grow. So neither the one who plants nor the one who waters is anything, but only God, who makes things grow" (1 Cor 3:7). Just like the farmer, all we can do is provide the conditions for spiritual development to happen. The right conditions, combined with the supernatural power and activity of God, bring about extraordinary spiritual change. Many of these conditions will be in place when you arrive at camp but as a leader you also will have a role in establishing an environment of spiritual growth. Here are the conditions staff can provide while partnering with God in the Christian camp environment:

Relationships are God's building blocks for his work on earth. Paul changes his analogy to the construction site: "No one can lay any foundation other than the one already laid, which is Jesus Christ. If anyone builds on this foundation using gold, silver, costly stones, wood, hay or straw, their work will be shown for what it is" (1 Cor 3:10-13). You get to build on campers' lives this summer, and the spiritual quality of your work matters! Through the love, patience and careful instruction of the Holy Spirit within you, eternal progress will be made; campers will respond first to you and then to the message of Jesus you proclaim. Be comprehensive in your relationships, avoiding the temptation to focus on the campers you most enjoy, and follow the example of Jesus the physician who came to serve those who needed him most.

The **Gospel** is "the power of God that brings salvation to everyone who believes" (Rom 1:16). God promises his spoken word will not return to him empty but will accomplish the purpose for which it was sent (Isa 55:10-11). There will be campers who hear God's word for the first time, and others who have been nearly drowned in it. As you plant the seed of the Gospel in their hearts, watch for signs of new life. If you neglect to bring them the word of God in a way they can hear and understand, don't expect very much (we will discuss this more later).

Most camp settings accentuate the natural wonder of **creation**. In fact, creation so reveals the nature of God that it leaves the unbeliever without excuse (Rom 1:18). The beauty of your setting or the bright night sky will make campers wonder and will raise the big questions of life. Be ready to make the most of the opportunities provided by the universe God shaped around us.

There is some level of **crisis** for everyone at camp. Whether it is being away from home for the first time or learning to wakeboard, the camp experience takes people out of their comfort zone. As a leader, you should help campers feel secure, but expect all these new and somewhat unsettling experiences to promote change in other areas of life. God often draws people to himself and strengthens their faith through troubling circumstances (1 Pet 1:6-9).

Hospitality creates an atmosphere of acceptance and belonging, a place where everyone knows one another's names. Jesus said, "Whoever welcomes a little child like this in my name welcomes me" (Matt 18:5). When you get down on one knee to greet a new camper who is half your size, you faithfully represent the heart of Jesus and create great first impressions: they are welcome here, you are glad to be their leader and they are safe with you.

Prayer makes all the difference in the camp setting. Join the many people praying for the ministry of your camp, and anticipate the activity of the Holy Spirit in response. Take every opportunity to pray with other staff, pray for other staff and ask for specific prayer from people at camp and at home. Pray for campers by name and ask God for specific circumstances to take place, so when he answers you will all know it. God does his work in an environment of prayer, moving through the expressed faith and desires of his people in community.

Through **miracles**, God affirms our many prayers with results only he could bring about. It may be as simple as finding a lost camera, as moving as watching a cold heart warmed to the Gospel or as spectacular as the shooting star a camper asked for in their heart. God makes known the veracity of the Gospel message through things that can only be explained as the work of God. Point out these affirmations to your campers.

All camp staff have a part in creating this environment of spiritual growth, but what will be your specific role? In a smaller camp setting, you may have a wide or varied set of responsibilities, from cabin leading to canoe instruction to worship leading. Larger settings allow you to specialize, though even then you will be expected to step into any role as needed. Even if you are asked to be the water boy, consider Jesus' words: "If anyone gives even a cup of cold water to one of these little ones who is my disciple, truly I tell you, that person will certainly not lose their reward" (Matt 10:42). No matter what your role, campers are watching. Your life can say, "Follow my example, as I follow the example of Christ" (1 Cor 11:1). In a support role, you may have time to focus on a camper when their cabin leader cannot. Here are some of the usual camp positions and what is expected of them.

Administrative staff include people such as the camp director and directors of various areas, head cabin leaders (or unit leaders or deans), office staff and leaders of training programs. For the most part, their primary responsibility is leading and looking after the rest of the staff team in very specific ways. They make decisions that set direction for the camp program and affect everyone, and they will appreciate your cooperation and prayers. Often they only deal directly with campers when issues come up that are beyond the ability of other staff. If you are one of the administrative staff, you will also need to make connections intentionally with campers, taking time out of your busy day to do so, or you might lose connection with the pulse of God's work in the cabin and playing field.

Support staff are those who serve in the kitchen and dishwashing room, the janitors and maintenance staff, and medical staff such as doctors, nurses or first aid attendants. They are called support staff because without them the work of cabin leaders, lifeguards and program leaders would be impossible. Because they work behind the scenes, they are easily taken for granted and will need relationship and consistent affirmation from other staff. If you are on support staff, you also need to look for ways of connecting directly with campers beyond serving them food and applying bandaids. For example, perhaps you could tell your story in a cabin one night, or help with a wide game.

Program staff run games and events, instruct and supervise recreational activities, lead worship or speak the word of God in chapel, or perhaps shoot photos or video to capture memories that campers can take home. In smaller camps, cabin leaders may run all the events and activities; larger camps will have staff who specialize. As program staff, you will have a key role in drawing kids to camp and making it a fun and memorable experience. Campers come with high expectations from the brochure or website or the stories of previous campers, and you won't want to disappoint them. Activities create many opportunities to build relationships and engage in significant conversations, including spiritual topics. Don't make the mistake of focusing so much on doing a great job as a wakeboard instructor that you miss the opportunity to model and talk about faith in Jesus.

Cabin leaders (called "counselors" at some camps) are the ones who have the most direct connection with campers. Years ago, summer camps found value in "decentralizing" their programs; that is, they moved away from large group events directed by a few leaders to small group activities led by many, which resulted in better personal attention, more interaction and other dynamics unique to small groups. The cabin leader will become the focus of this book as we turn our attention to the specific skills and responsibilities of this position.

Many cabin leaders come to camp for just one week of the summer, admirably giving up a week of vacation each year to pour heart and soul into a group of campers—perhaps the same ones for several years in a row. It is a very full and exciting week! Whether you are serving for one week or several, don't approach cabin-leading like a 100-meter dash; you will need to pace yourself like a marathon runner. Exhaustion will distance you from your campers and diminish your thoughtfulness and creativity. As much as possible, leave margins of time and energy for yourself; you can't possibly know what is around the corner. Make use of your support crew—the head cabin leaders, directors and others who are there to encourage you.

As a cabin leader, obviously you will need to provide **leadership**. Legally, as a cabin leader you are acting *in loco parentis*, "in the place of a parent," which means you need to provide the care and supervision that a reasonable parent would if they were there. Campers want to have confidence in you, so be assertive and decisive when they look to you for direction. At the same time, speak and act with gentleness and respect, keeping in mind the servant-leadership of Jesus. Pray for the wisdom you will need to make decisions in the best interest of your campers.

You are the one who should shape the **group dynamics** in your cabin. Early on, create a sense of group identity among your campers by doing things no other cabin does: choose a cabin song; dress up for a meal; stage a flashmob in the middle of the field. Seek to give each camper an identity and a way to contribute to the group: make the natural leader in the cabin your assistant; let the shy one carry the team flag in the wide game. Encourage and affirm, and give campers opportunity to do the same with one another.

Much of your time will be taken up with **management**. You are the supervisor of each camper's schedule, the manager of their stuff and the umpire as you deal with issues and problems. It matters more how you manage your campers than what your management accomplishes. A super neat and tidy cabin is of no importance if it is the result of intimidation; winning the talent night doesn't cut it if you should have taken time to help a camper find his lost running shoes. It is absolutely essential you know where your campers are or should be at all times. Take every opportunity to count your sheep: first thing in the morning and last at night; at every meal and snack time, chapel and fireside; at the start of every activity and after your time at the waterfront. Don't let it pass if one is missing: leave the 99 with someone and find your one lost lamb! Make your campers aware of the schedule to help keep absences to a minimum.

The younger the camper, the more basic **physical care** is needed; the older the camper, the more example is needed. Young campers won't think to wash their hands between the BMX track and the lunch table. They leave things behind and may not even remember what belongs to them until you show them their name on the label. Older campers may resent over-careful instruction as an insult to their maturity, but they may still forget to use deodorant until they see you using yours.

Cabin leaders provide **spiritual care**. More than anyone, you have an opportunity to teach campers from the word of God. Make the most of it in every setting and watch their spiritual progress. The God element is all new for some of your campers, and your actions will speak more clearly than your words. Others need to be shaken from their spiritual complacency and automatic answers through challenging questions and new ways of looking at things. Ask God for the discernment to see each camper's spiritual condition, a vision of what they could become and the wisdom to nudge them in this direction.

Now you know what you will do as a cabin leader, but what will the week look like? The weekly schedule will vary from camp to camp, but there are some standard features you can expect. The **first day** has interesting dynamics—just put yourself in a camper's shoes! You may have started thinking about camp just a few days before; maybe the trip to camp was long and filled with anticipation or apprehension. Whatever happens in those first few moments at camp forms the lens through which campers will see the rest of the week. Misinterpretation is probable. That is why staff need to work so hard to create a good first impression. Greet them with warmth and enthusiasm: "I've been watching for you!" or "I am so glad you are in my cabin." Memorize names quickly, show interest in getting to know them and help them get established and oriented. The first day of camp can be hectic, but take short periods of time to give each of your campers 100% of your attention, and get them interacting with one another. Be prepared with ways to bond your cabin—paint their faces, have a squirt gun battle or teach them a new circle game—which will help each one find their place in the group. Focus on the campers, but don't ignore lingering parents either—thank them for trusting you with their child, and ask if there is anything you should know.

The camp will probably determine the time for **lights out** at the end of the day, but it will be up to you as the cabin leader to help campers wind down and get to sleep. After an active night game, followed by hot chocolate and cookies, bedtime can be difficult! Your campers cannot just flip a switch and shut down. Help them make the transition: from moving to talking; from talking to listening; from listening to sleeping. You can make good use of this time, as you will see when we talk about leading discussions on the Bible. Start with an activity that has a point to it, then a discussion about something from the word of God, and finish up with a related story (maybe your story). Still wide awake? Rather than let them wind up again, draw from your repertoire of long stories and riddles (avoid horror and tragedy— you don't know the background of your campers!). Even a super-secret mission in the dark (pre-arranged, of course) can do a surprisingly good job of helping them wind down. Sometimes a great discussion is a reason to stay up late, but be careful not to over-influence campers through sleep deprivation.

Wake-up should be gentle. For some kids, a bad start to the day just means a bad day, so be sensitive to campers who aren't "morning people." Younger campers are likely to get up very early on the first morning of camp. Be prepared with something you can do with them (besides growl) in the hours before breakfast: a walk, a snack, a cabin game, morning exercises or a challenge.

Mealtimes need a good balance of fun and control. Try to be the initiator of fun ideas at mealtimes, rather than always squelching the campers' ideas of fun. Talk opera style throughout the meal, or wear towels on your heads and pretend to be Bedouins. Avoid wasting food or doing activities that will take away their appetites. You are the only one making sure your campers are maintaining a healthy diet. Away from a parent's supervision, some campers will take the opportunity to overeat, or not eat enough. If you suspect a camper has a serious eating problem, seek help from camp leadership rather than trying to manage the situation on your own.

Cabin time may be part of your camp's schedule or may occur due to bad weather. Hopefully you brought some great small group activity ideas: hold a cabin Olympics event with straw javelins and pebble shot-put; play human tic-tac-toe; try team-building games like lining up alphabetically without talking to one another; play "I Spy" or "Hotter and Colder" or charades; have a cabin talent show or do improvised theatre sports. If the purpose of cabin time is to clean the cabin, make it your goal not only to make it spotless but a more pleasant place to live. Be a good model for your campers, and never be the cause of losing clean-up points for your cabin!

Most Christian camps have regular **chapel sessions** or **firesides**, with a worship band leader and a speaker or cabin discussions. For many kids at camp, Bible discussions and worship are entirely foreign; others may have heard it all before and not pay attention. The best way to interest both kinds of campers in spiritual instruction is to carry them along with your own interest, involvement and enthusiasm. You can help campers focus on what is being taught by staying focused yourself. If possible, sit with your campers so you can watch for their response to the music, the speaking and the discussion, which may open up further conversations with them. Firesides have a way of focusing people's attention and creating an atmosphere of acceptance and openness. They can also be emotionally charged, so be sure to follow up a camper's response at fireside with conversation in another setting so her decision will go beyond an emotional response.

At many camps, cabin leaders are also the instructors for **recreational activities**. Kids come to camp primarily for the fun and relationships; leaders at camp have to keep in mind several other important factors. The Christian camp is about discipleship, and recreation provides shared experiences, relationships and metaphors about trust. Some camps place emphasis on certification in outdoor skills, or character development and confidence through adventure activities; others are more about social interaction and play. Safety is a primary concern, balancing the perceived risk of exciting activities with the real risks involved, whether emotionally or physically. Camps tend to invest a great deal of time and resources into their recreational activities, but it is the leader's enthusiasm and engagement that will create the great memories.

Games and team competition are a large part of many camp programs. Whether you help lead games and events, or simply participate with your campers, your purpose remains the same: to make the game the best possible experience for the campers. A cabin leader who has too much adrenaline pumping while playing a game can be hazardous to the emotional and physical health of campers, and his own. Games often require careful explanations, and you can help the leader by keeping your campers focused and by listening carefully so you understand the game yourself. If the game begins to slow down or campers lose interest, your energy and enthusiasm will carry the day. Gather a few campers together and make a sacrificial, major assault. Watch for kids who are too shy or too cool to get involved and take them with you. Even if it means losing, encourage the campers to be creative and to do the important stuff in the game rather than doing it for them. Above all, don't give in to the temptation to cheat, which can undo much of your hard work of discipleship.

There may be several **special events** during the week, such as a skit or talent night, a banquet, dramatic productions, dress-up-the-leader events and the like. Though you will usually have to be the catalyst for your cabin's ideas and get them started, try to promote your campers' creativity as much as possible. Avoid compromise when your campers beg to do something you (and the camp leadership) would consider rude, violent or offensive, and decide beforehand whether or not you will allow them to shave your head! These can be some of your best opportunities to build group dynamics and create memories, so put your heart and effort into these events.

Some of the most important moments at camp are the **in-between times**, the breathing space between activities or before and after a meal. Camps are wise to increase these important spaces as the week progresses to allow campers to reflect on their experiences, interact with staff and respond in some meaningful way. Use these times well. A significant conversation with a camper might come about after everyone else has rushed out of the dining hall and you are alert enough to notice this camper is not in a rush. Excitement and noise are good and essential parts of camp, but they need to be punctuated by a little hush once in a while so we can pause to understand what camp is all about. So when God whispers, we will still hear him.

In-between times are also potential opportunities for trouble. Campers in transition are harder to supervise and are often creating their own entertainment. At the same time, some staff tend to use in-between times as open space for themselves, perhaps to talk together, use the washroom, see the nurse or whatever. This seems only reasonable, but the potential for problems is obvious. These are the times fights break out, homesickness erupts, vandalism occurs and accidents happen. As much as reasonably possible, be among campers during the times before and after meals, while everyone is waking up or going to bed and between programmed activities. Be alert to problems, and don't hesitate to step in.

It is imperative the cabin leader is fully present on the **last day** of camp. Camp is not over until it is over! It is crucial you remain available to your campers until the last one is gone. This is tricky because you have things to do that day—pack up, clean the cabin, reunite lost and found items with campers—but this is also the time when a camper might finally be ready to open up about something or ask about the Gospel. As much as possible, save your personal tasks until after they leave, which can also be a good time to reflect on the week and release your campers into Jesus' care. Make it your goal to spend a few individual moments with every one of your campers. Pray and ask God to make you especially sensitive and approachable. Be there when it is time for each camper to leave—those tears on the last day speak of the significance of what happened during their week.

Jesus called himself the "Good Shepherd" who knows his sheep and is known by them (John 10). Unlike the hired hand, who doesn't care for the sheep and abandons them when the wolf comes, Jesus is the owner of the sheep and so he lays down his life for them. I pray this summer you will take ownership of the ministry of your camp and of the children and youth under your care. This is much, much more than a summer job.

<u>Think about this:</u>
- What are your camp's specific expectations of you this summer?
- What questions do you need to ask friends who have been in your position before, or ask the camp leadership directly?
- Who have you asked to pray for you every day of your week at camp?

"And God is able to make all grace abound to you, so that having all sufficiency in all things at all times, you may abound in every good work" (2 Cor 9:8).

PART TWO: I WANT TO SEE EVERY
CAMPER THROUGH JESUS' EYES

5. Understand and Love Kids

How did Jesus view people? There are clues in the Bible that are helpful for us to consider. We are told that our Creator "does not look at the things people look at. People look at the outward appearance, but the Lord looks at the heart" (1 Sam 16:7). The religious leaders recognized that Jesus was not swayed by people, because he paid no attention to their station in life (Matt 22:16). Paul took up Jesus' example: "As for those who were held in high esteem —whatever they were makes no difference to me; God does not show favoritism—they added nothing to my message" (Gal 2:6). Image, status and performance did not affect the way Jesus viewed and interacted with each person who came into his circle.

Camp lends itself to a similar level playing field, a place where one's image on Facebook and grades at school don't matter. Because of the expense of camp, kids tend to come primarily from privileged families, or from underprivileged families whose fees are subsidized. As leaders who follow Jesus, we will be careful not to focus on the advantaged or the cool kids at the expense of the marginalized. There will also be a range of different personalities among your campers, so if you are an extrovert you should not assume there is something wrong with a camper who would rather read a book than join the dance party. We need to see campers as individuals, each uniquely formed in character and personality by our Creator, developing uniquely from their particular background and circumstances. We need to see them with Jesus' eyes.

You may think that, as a younger person, you already understand what it is like to be a 13-year-old kid these days. It is a common misconception of adults. Really, so much has changed in the past five years that you would be surprised at the current issues young campers are facing. Even the young teens you think you know so well are hiding things that would surprise you, an underworld of relationships, values, language and loyalties (Chap Clark, *Hurt 2.0: Inside the World of Today's Teenagers*, 2011). But there are some patterns among kids and teens that will help us understand them better and respond to their needs. It is good to explore these generalities without losing our interest in the specific characteristics and needs of the individual. Let's take a tour through the years of life represented by the children and youth who most often come to camp, ages seven to eighteen.

Seven is a pretty early age to come to camp on your own. Some camps offer shorter programs for this and even younger ages, and it is often the children's first experience away from home without their parents. These children are very dependent; they need to be reminded to brush their teeth and find it hard to go to sleep without the usual nightstomach stomach time rituals. Going to the bathroom, washing up before meals and getting ready for bed become small group events, done together. You will need to manage their basic need for rest, appropriately provide affection, keep expectations uncomplicated and be genuine in your enthusiasm. At this age simple is better and easy is fun. This is still an age of testing the boundaries, and they seek the security of defined rules and limited space. If these are not provided, children—especially as a group—cannot be expected to have the maturity to stop pushing. Children are not too young for spiritual understanding; Jesus prayed, "I praise you, Father, Lord of heaven and earth, because you have hidden these things from the wise and learned, and revealed them to little children" (Matt 11:25). Be supportive of their spiritual response at this young age, but don't offer them so much special attention that you suddenly have the whole cabin wanting to respond simply to please you.

If you have the opportunity to work with the **eight to ten** age group you will find them very excitable and responsive to everything you do, but you may start to panic when you realize that your campers' energy is new every morning while your own is not. Though they may have come with friends, this age group's week at camp will revolve around their cabin leader. What an opportunity! Perhaps you are the final person to have this kind of influence with these campers before they plunge into the ordeal of adolescence. These campers still see life as a series of snapshots—isolated, consecutive events—and so they have a conclusion on practically every area of life and will talk constantly about things of which they have little knowledge or experience. Are you interested in their chatter? Probably not, but consider what you communicate to them when you take time to listen: "You are worth my time and attention. I am glad to be here with you. I care about you."

Don't blow it by cheating in a game—their linear thinking makes fairness one of their strongest values. Campers of this age also have a great capacity for learning and memorization, and for the most part still enjoy the challenge. Whether it is part of your camp's program or not, make the most of the opportunity to memorize verses from the Bible together and hide them in their hearts. You can't possibly give to these campers all the time and attention they will demand of you—there is simply not enough of you to go around. Instead of trying to give all of them some of your attention all the time, which will frustrate both you and your campers, give each one all of your attention for short bursts of time.

The crisis of puberty overtakes most campers at some point from age **ten to thirteen**, which is why in the same camp there are little boys and small women. In a society that ridicules rather than celebrates the changes taking place in a pre-teen, adolescence can be a frightening and lonely perplexity. As they begin to think abstractly, they no longer process the circumstances of life as individual events; they now see patterns in those events and begin to make troubling conclusions about themselves and the world around them. Their sense of identity begins to shift from parents to peers as they learn that they must fit in to avoid becoming a target of gossip or bullying. There is a growing tension between what they have been taught all their lives and what they see and hear in the world, and their parents' influence loses ground.

Self-consciousness limits their choices and abbreviates their words. They begin to blame themselves for the bad things that happen to them, not because it makes sense but so they can stay in control and not let those things happen again. As a result, they have a greater tendency to make destructive choices and so repeat the cycle (Marv Penner, *Help My Kids Are Hurting*, 2005). It is a difficult time. Can you see how important it is for their camp leader to listen without judgment, and offer understanding rather than pat answers or advice? These young hearts are raw, but are also open and seeking. Take them to Jesus, with gentleness and respect.

The next few years from **thirteen to fifteen** are a tumultuous period of testing and rethinking everything. The assumptions they once held now lie scattered behind them and they will spend the next several years piecing it all together again. As a camp leader, they may not trust you right away, but patient and respectful persistence will often find its way past the defenses of a teen by the middle of the week. Many teens have learned to distance themselves from adults by flaunting their issues, or protect themselves by taking their issues underground; if you can hang in there and show them you will not give up on them, they will love you for it.

These campers value being part of a group of friends—though it is not unusual for them to move in or out of a circle of friends for any reason—and that group highly influences their choices while they are in it. You may find it more effective to work with these shifting friendship groups than work against them. Of course, our culture intensifies the influence of friends by making moral boundaries so vague or by refusing to set them at all. Thankfully, many of these campers have had enough childhood direction, personal integrity and pure grace from God not to push the boundaries too far even though they know they could. Many adults are appalled at the immorality of youth; I am amazed at how moral they are considering the opportunities they have to be immoral, and I wonder how well most adults would do in their shoes. Still, this is a fragile age, and I have seen simple hurt feelings turn into disappointment, rebellion and disaster. The cabin leader of this age group needs to pray for wisdom, compassion and patience.

By the time they reach the age of **sixteen to eighteen**, campers begin to make firm choices about their values, beliefs, principles, interests, passions and the friends they will keep. They are pursuing independence, and so they value freedom of choice above everything else. This can be challenging for the cabin leader who wants to respect their maturity yet sees areas where they still need guidance and boundaries. These campers are adopting opinions and lifestyles that are very important to them, and that you may find very distressing. Argument and condemnation will not help you, nor will silence and tolerance. Listening and prayerful response is more effective. Compassion and example drew the secularized crowds to Jesus, and through you his Spirit can speak to the hearts of young adults whose worldview is like wet concrete soon to set.

As they determine what matters to them in life, these campers begin planning and working seriously toward significant achievements. At this age, they are bored when they sense that what they are doing has no significance and achieves nothing that matters to them. Camp needs to be a significant experience, worth taking a week off the summer job. Many young adults are drawn to the idea of becoming camp staff because it offers more opportunity and responsibility than they would ever be given back home. Camp is a closed system, like a rock climber on belay taking chances that would not be safe in other settings, and the adventure of it all is very appealing to an emerging adult.

Your camp may also offer a program for **families**. Adults arrive at camp with large expectations of what this week will do for their families—sometimes unreasonable ones. They may not realize how stressed and tired they are until the pace of camp begins to slow them down. They too need Jesus, and the role of staff is no less important than ever. In my experience, what family campers seem to appreciate most about camp is the staff's investment in their kids and their encouraging example. Is that not the way it should be? Paul said, "Don't let anyone look down on you because you are young, but set an example for the believers in speech, in conduct, in love, in faith and in purity" (1 Tim 4:12). Be careful not to give them any reason to look down on you, like waking up their kids as you talk and laugh on your way to bed at midnight. Family campers are at camp for a holiday and have invested time and money to be there. But they also need discipleship and can come to follow your example as you follow the example of Christ.

At risk of becoming obsolete before this is even published, can we take a look at the world in which these campers are growing up? Even the youngest are feeling the effects of family instability, as more marriages fall apart in North America than succeed. Misbehavior is the evidence you might witness in children with precarious family situations, but the root cause of their behavior is likely strong and suppressed emotion—anger, guilt and fear— expressed in disruptive actions because no one is paying them any attention. Children are also exposed at younger ages than ever to adult vices: sexual images, vocabulary, experimentation and abuse; recreational drugs and alcohol; violence, vandalism and shoplifting. Pressure from peers and older children to experiment can begin as soon as they start school, or even in the daycare. Media adds to the pressure, telling them from a young age that physical appearance is the measure of their worth, sex is recreational, sexual orientation is arbitrary, people are dispensable and violence is an acceptable solution. Bullying takes on new forms as pre-teens begin to access social networking such as Facebook and Snapchat, utilizing cruel words and unfair images to shame, shun and even blackmail their victims. This is especially hurtful as they get older because image has become everything to them, as it has to most adults.

Image makes or breaks their social standing, whether or not there is any substance behind it. For example, some outstanding young adults have resorted to self-injury, substance abuse or even suicide because of the consequences of having their image destroyed online. Who they really were was overwritten by what people looking at a web browser thought of them. What a strange world.

People coming to camp are hurting more than they let on. Technology magnifies the pain because in spite of instant communication we have a sense that no one is really listening, that no one has any understanding of how we actually feel. How did Jesus respond to hurting people? He gave them his time and attention. He loved them just as they were, but refused to leave them as they were. We can do the same, by moving every camper forward in their walk with God! What an amazing opportunity you have before you this summer.

Think about this:

- How about memorizing the above characteristics for the age group you will serve at camp?
- How ready are you to give your heart away to a group of needy kids this summer?

6. Build Relationships and Community

As mentioned, relationships are the building material of God's work here on earth. Jesus said the two most important things in life are to love God and love our neighbor (Matt 22:37-40). Through relationships, God peopled the world, described himself to us, communicated his will, defeated sin and death and established his kingdom. God himself is a relationship, a unique and mysterious unity of three Persons in one Being: the Triune God.

After serving at the same camp for many years, I had the opportunity to watch some campers grow up and become staff. They often contact me about a problem or to ask for a reference letter. What amazes me is that we have developed a trust relationship in a very short time, which says there is something unique and powerful about the relationships created at camp.

People at camp get to know one another very well,

very fast. The tears on the last day are real, but it is more like seeing the movie than reading the book. There is much about your campers you will not get to know, and the memories fade quickly. Younger campers will trust you immediately simply because of your staff t-shirt; older campers may be suspicious of any adult who wants to spend time with them, as this has not always gone well for them in the past. It is good to examine your own motives for this relationship: Are you initiating friendship because it is your job, or as a sneaky means of sharing the Gospel, or is your love for the camper genuine, no strings attached? Take Paul's example in his ministry: "Because we loved you so much, we were delighted to share with you not only the gospel of God but our lives as well" (1 Thes 2:8).

The most significant thing you can do for your campers in one week is to get to know them and allow them to get to know you. There are some tried and proven ways of building good relationships with kids that you will do well to practice:

Make it your goal to **learn their names** by dinnertime on the first day of camp. You know what it feels like when someone who should know your name forgets. You should know their names; bad memory is no excuse. You will need to make a conscious decision to memorize their names as you meet them; use their name as you talk with them, and your mind will begin to associate their name with their face. It may be helpful to try other associations as well: you met "Sandy" at the beach; "Matt" has a welcoming look on his face (sorry!). Whenever you can, silently look around the circle and rehearse their names. It doesn't take long, and it means much to them.

Pay attention. This is hard for us in a world in which we fill up every empty moment with distractions, but hopefully, your cell phone is not in your pocket at camp. When a camper is on your radar, give her your 100% undistracted attention until it is time to move on, showing her she is your first priority for that moment. If you have younger campers mobbing you for attention all the time, be the initiator of attention rather than the defender of your sanity—go out of your way to give a camper a hug for no reason, or ask him a question or his opinion, leaving the 99 to fend for themselves for a while. Campers will soon come to realize your attention is offered freely and generously, but not when they beg for it.

To guard one-on-one conversations from awkwardness, add a **third something** to the conversation to relieve the tension. It can be a bag of chips to share or looking at the view, a ping-pong table between you or sitting by the campfire. Campers will often feel more comfortable speaking in the dark of the cabin at night, or while walking with you down a path.

As much as possible, make yourself **available and approachable**. The camp schedule can keep you moving from place to place all day; when you pause regularly, you open up spaces for campers to spend time with you and talk. Maybe you don't need to get up and leave the very moment lunch is over; perhaps thirty more seconds at the campfire will be noticed by a camper who hoped to talk with you. I imagine Jesus

THE CHRISTIAN CAMP LEADER

this way—not in a hurry, but rather one of those rare people who has time for other people. Use body language that tells campers your store is open: get off your cell phone, talk with that cute staff member another time, welcome a passing camper with eye contact and a smile—an unusual occurrence in their experience with most adults.

Look for **common ground** with your campers. John Thomas tells us of his traumatic first arrival at camp, sitting on a bunk across from his cabin leader: "I wondered what he could possibly say to make me feel better. 'So, John, do you have a dog?' Those seven simple words began a friendship that would last many years—and start me on my long journey of healing" (*Boundless Webzine*, July 2000). Beyond the (limited) common interests you have with your campers, create common ground out of the shared experiences of the day. Take time each evening to tell one another the stories of the day; make events into memories. You don't need to become a kid again, but also don't expect things of your campers you are unwilling to carry out yourself—do the actions to the songs, be goofy on skit night. Find every available connection with your campers. Paul's philosophy was to "become all things to all people so that by all possible means I might save some" (1 Cor 9:22).

Consistency is key to the progress of your relationships. Cabin leaders' best efforts have been destroyed by a careless word spoken to another staff member while unaware that a camper is in the bathroom stall next to them. Campers need regular affirmations of your interest in them and apologies when you mess up. Favoritism is contrary to the law of Christ (James 2:8-9), who died for us when we were still sinners. Don't let a week of camp go by before you realize there is a camper who has received almost no attention from you, while others have been your obvious preference.

Be kind, in word and deed. Some kids can't handle teasing or sarcasm, which is all they get at home. Use words to affirm and encourage and challenge; "Do not let any unwholesome talk come out of your mouths, but only what is helpful for building others up according to their needs, that it may benefit those who listen" (Eph 4:29). Thoughtfulness requires planning ahead to do for campers what you would want to be done if you were in their shoes. Leave that note on their pillow; bring the stuffed mascot they will remember you for; include a snack in your evening discussion time. Help campers with their luggage on the first day—it makes me burn inside watching a little kid struggle with a suitcase while following an empty-handed cabin leader. Imitate the kindness of our Savior.

As a leader after the heart of Jesus, **humility** is essential in your relationships with your campers. Paul's words to the church are a good rule of thumb: "Live in harmony with one another. Do not be proud, but be willing to associate with people of low position [alternately: *be willing to do menial work*]. Do not be conceited" (Rom 12:16). Harmony will rule in your cabin when you set aside your own agenda and look out for the best interests of your campers. This was the mindset of Jesus as he came to live among us (Phil 2:5-8). Make every effort to be comprehensive in your relationships; leave no one out. Be the first to volunteer for the undesirable task, and grab the ugliest lifejacket for yourself. If you hurt a camper with a careless word or thoughtless act, apologize as soon as you can and make it right with her.

Tim Hansel says that what kids need most from the adults in their lives is **enthusiasm** (*What Kids Need Most in a Dad*, 2002), because enthusiasm communicates love and appreciation. The noisiest team is always the winner at camp, at least in my books. Cabin leaders who go all out for their campers are heroes of the faith, sacrificing energy and their voices for the cause of the kingdom. Well, don't hurt yourself—but do let your campers know how much they mean to you by being fully engaged in the program, getting excited about their smallest triumph. God is said to delight in us and rejoice over us with singing (Zeph 3: 17). He is an enthusiastic God, and so are his children.

There are campers who will not easily respond to your best efforts, and your **perseverance** will be important. Remember how far Jesus went to love the unlovable, heal those whom society had cast out and forgive those whose sins were many. Don't give up easily on a camper or write her off as an enemy. She is watching your persistence carefully; she is testing the boundaries to see if your offer of friendship is real. Even if the week passes with no evident response, your faithfulness has spoken volumes to her about the God whom you serve, and she may tell people back home it was the best week of her life. Be faithful, and leave the results to God.

In the camp setting, relationship building is more

than a one-on-one exercise. You are also developing community with your campers. I have observed three characteristics of a healthy temporary community in the cabin group at camp. They may surprise you.

Inclusiveness. I have watched some cabin leaders work very hard at becoming exclusive with their cabin. They become very competitive and sneer at the attempts of others to match them. They are constantly out of sync with the program as they do their own thing. The group becomes very self-focused and ineffective for the purposes of God. Transform your perception of the cabin group from a private social club to an absorbing community. Group dynamics become exclusive—and unhealthy—when they are self-serving; the inclusive group has an excitement to share what they have. The early church was described as a group no one else dared to join, yet more and more people believed and were added to their number (Acts 5:12-14). How did that happen? It was inclusive—the church drew into itself the people around them to share in the great thing they were experiencing. As cabin leader, you can model and nurture that attitude: inviting the janitor to share his story in your cabin; picking up the strays in the night game; letting other campers and staff into your circle on the field.

Transparency. Everyone wants to be heard. Even the shyest person wants deep down to be noticed, to know someone is paying attention. But too much openness has also hurt all of us before, and whether due to wisdom gained or resulting inhibitions, we are to one degree or another guarded in what we say—especially about ourselves. The small cabin group is

THE CHRISTIAN CAMP LEADER

one of those relatively safe places where campers begin to open up about themselves, and this transparency can be a sign of the group's health. As a cabin leader, you have the opportunity and responsibility to ensure your group cultivates an atmosphere of openness and responds well to those who speak out. What a camper says about himself may be like a loaded gun placed in the hands of his cabin group. Will the group use his words against him —or perhaps even worse, disregard them—or will it respond with love, concern, encouragement and affirmation? Always give campers opportunity to respond to one another, but model and encourage a positive response, even if what was shared was negative or painful.

Ownership. You can easily tell when members of a cabin group begin to have a sense of ownership of their group. It is the cabin that cheers for their teammates even when they come in last; they stand up for one another against all threats; you see them hanging out together in spite of differences in their interests and social standing. The tricky thing for a cabin leader is to develop this sense of ownership without it becoming exclusive and competitive. Have pride in the group without distancing or comparing yourselves to other groups. Campers with ownership will have a sense of belonging and will know their unique role in the cabin group. They not only take an interest in one another; they bear one another's burdens. Their love for one another covers over a multitude of sins that would otherwise become irritants. In the condensed experience of camp, this dynamic can grow in a matter of days, as cabin leaders model and cultivate a healthy environment. Just as

God works through community dynamics in the church, he will work in big ways through the community you cultivate at camp.

Sometimes the dynamics in your cabin will be difficult. You may end up with two separate groups of friends that decide not to like one another, or groups of friends plus one camper who came on his own and feels left out. Especially with older campers, you will need to work hard to give a voice to that one lonely camper or create shared experiences that will draw them together. Sometimes a natural leader will arise among the campers; don't let her become your enemy or you may find the whole group against you. Build trust: give that person a role of responsibility in the group that will bring them onside.

When relationship-building is your fulltime job, you expose yourself to a great deal of risk. Are you ready to have your heart stretched and even broken? C.S. Lewis wrote that to love is to be vulnerable—and likely you will be hurt—but the only alternative is a cold and impenetrable heart (*The Four Loves*, 1960). God knew before he created the world that it would mean the sacrifice of his own Son, and he created us anyway. Jump in with both feet, give your heart to this group of small people, and you will find it worth the price.

Think about this:
- What items will you bring with you to help develop cabin identity?

7. Help Campers Discover Truth

Everything you do in a day as a cabin leader is spiritually charged. Let's imagine you had some time this afternoon to pull together a great little evening Bible discussion for your campers. As you finally get them settled down that night on the floor of the cabin, time stands still for a moment and several scenes flash in front of your eyes: at breakfast you had two muffins and Mike didn't get one; your buddy at the dock snuck you into the wakeboard lineup ahead of Brad and he didn't get to go; Phil and Ben are still mad at you over the toilet paper incident; and you can't remember any significant conversation so far with Matt, Dave or Jon. Okay, you did have a great time tossing a Frisbee with Sam, which led to an interesting talk about his messed up family situation. But you are suddenly less excited about your lesson plan.

The point is, you teach your campers all day long, not just when you open your Bible with them half an hour before lights out. What they learn from your interactions in a day has much more weight than your few words that evening (Gladys Hunt, "How to Lead Small Group Bible Studies with Campers", CCCA *Focus Series*). It doesn't mean that teaching them from the Bible is a waste of time; instead, what you teach them from the Bible should recap what you have taught them all day. Whether your camp gives you specific directions and materials to use, or just leaves spiritual instruction up to you, make the most of every opportunity to teach your campers from your understanding and practice of the word of God, whether it is at the end of a chapel session or on the volleyball court.

That said, you will likely have opportunities to lead campers in planned Bible discussions. Does that scare you? Or maybe you can't wait to have a small, captive audience for your half-hour sermon! Let's try another option: interactive discussions that come from the overflow of your own study of the word of God.

Earlier, I mentioned the spiritual discipline of interpretation, which is reading the word of God with the intention of understanding what it says, what it means and what you will do about it. This is for your own sake but also for the benefit of those you will teach. The time to begin your preparation for this summer's cabin discussions is now—with your consistent reading, study and practice of the word of God. Then your discussions will flow from your heart, not just from a scrap of notepaper. As you read the word, prayerfully take note (maybe in a journal) of the specifics the Holy Spirit points out to you, such as fresh ideas that never caught your attention before or concepts that raise questions for you. Then for each passage you study, discover the "big idea" God is saying to you, the main concept to take with you into the world. During the day, bring that idea into focus again and again; let it permeate your thoughts and shape your actions.

You just did 90% of your cabin discussion preparation.

Prepping a Bible discussion is like buying a sandwich at one of those places where they make it right in front of you. Your personal study of the Bible has laid out all the items you need for your discussion with campers; now you just need to put it all together.

Imagine I invited you to the sandwich shop and asked: what will you have? Your mouth is watering for a Reuben—pastrami, swiss cheese, sauerkraut and loads of veggies. On multigrain. I commend you for your choice, but then tell the sandwich lady we are going to have our sandwiches without bread today. Since the insides are the most important part, who needs bread? She looks at us funny, but dutifully piles up the meat, veggies and sauerkraut and wraps it up for you. It is a soggy little package, dripping sauerkraut juice. Served this way, your appetite is suddenly gone.

The same thing will happen if you start your Bible discussion by saying, "Everyone turn to Habakkuk 3 —Katie, can you read the first five verses for us?" The Bible is the most important part of your discussion, but you may find your campers have no appetite for it served this way. What if instead I order you the multigrain bread but no pastrami or anything else to go inside? That is no good either: a "Bible" discussion without the Bible will be empty and ineffective, no matter how interesting you try to make it.

Let's build a great discussion sandwich, based on a familiar passage: Philippians 4:6-7 (note: this is the easy to read NIrV translation, so let's imagine you are preparing this for younger campers). "Don't worry about anything. Instead, tell God about everything. Ask and pray. Give thanks to him. Then God's peace will watch over your hearts and your minds because you belong to Christ Jesus. God's peace can never be completely understood."

The bun part of a sandwich is really just a tasty container for all the juicy goodness inside. Our discussion starts with a **bottom bun**, which is something that will invite campers to discover the truth of God's word. It may be a story, a game, a role-play or something else that is appealing enough to grab your cabin's attention. For our passage, I will collect enough smooth stones from the beach for each camper to have one, borrow pencils from the office and start our discussion with examples of things I sometimes worry about, which will hopefully lead the campers to share their anxieties. I will ask them to write as many of their worries as they can on their stone.

The **top bun** will be similar but will help campers decide what to do about what they have learned. Our prayers will be very active tonight because at the end of our discussion we will go down to the lake with our worry stones and throw them as far as we can into the water.

Now we have a tasty container that draws campers into discussion and leads them to action. Let's fill it!

The **meat and veggies** of our discussion are the concepts contained in the Bible passage; combined together they produce a flavor that we will call **The Big Idea**. The concepts I notice in our passage are: stop worrying; tell God about everything; thank him for everything; God's peace will guard you; you can leave your worries in God's hands. We can sum these up with The Big Idea, "Turn your worries into prayers." This is the concept we pray campers will understand, remember and put into practice.

The next consideration is how to lead your campers to The Big Idea without simply handing it to them. Why? It is important for campers to **discover** the truth of God's word. You could simply tell them all the concepts you found in Philippians 4 and sum it up with your astounding Big Idea. But the next morning, I bet not one of your campers will remember your rousing sermon. People are much more likely to remember and take to heart what they discover for themselves. How will you help them accomplish that?

Ask them questions.

They need to be the right kind of questions. Here's a real discussion-stopper: "So, what do you think this verse means?" That is the kind of question that makes kids roll their eyes, swing from the rafters and make rude body noises. And the boys are even worse. The question is so general any answer will do and no one will want to offer one. Make your questions specific: "Why does God want you to thank him for stuff that makes you worried?" Also, ask questions that make them look in their Bible for answers: "What do you think happens inside us when we pray?" Keep in mind that if you are looking for the right answer, it is no longer a discussion; it's a test. Ask for opinions, and respond graciously to opinions different from your own. Some of the best questions have no question marks: "Tell me about a time when you were very afraid and talked to God about it."

In a typical cabin discussion, you should ask 6-8 questions that focus on the Bible passage, in addition to any questions that are included in your bun (consider those ones mayonnaise or honey mustard). The questions should be designed to lead your campers to explore the passage and discover The Big Idea, so it is best to write them down ahead of time. But as you teach, stay flexible to the questions and needs of your campers, and especially to the leading of the Holy Spirit. After all, it is his Book you are teaching!

So there it is: a complete discussion sandwich! Sorry if all this talk about food made you hungry. Start with the bottom bun (talk about worries and write on the stones), pile on your meat-and-veggie questions from Philippians 4 (aim for The Big Idea: turn your worries into prayers) and finish with the top bun (throw the stones in the water as a form of prayer).

One of the best ways to help your campers respond to what they have learned is to encourage them to pray out loud. Some less intimidating ways of doing this include "popcorn prayer" (campers call out one word to finish a prayer such as "God, you are...") and prayer questions ("If you could ask God for one thing, what would it be?"). Keep your own prayers simple, and you will be surprised how many campers are willing to follow your example.

It is possible your camp will give you discussion materials to use, and you may think—great, I don't have to do any preparation at all! I want to caution you that prep is still needed so you will know what you are talking about and so you don't end up leading something that makes you and your campers less than happy. At a minimum, find the Bible passage(s) in the material and study them on your own. Look through the discussion questions and determine if your campers will get into them. Then, as you lead, use the material as a guide, not a script. Make it your own. Your camp will be okay with your creative use of the material, as long as you take your campers to the same Big Idea as everyone else.

Begin any Bible discussion with prayer, asking God to speak to all of you through his word. As you are leading the discussion, the voices of the campers should be heard about as much as yours, as you ask questions and they respond. Use good listening skills, like eye contact, focused attention and responses that prompt more talking—"Can you give me an example of what you mean?" or "How did you feel about what happened?" Maintain an atmosphere of acceptance; you are not looking for the "right" answer, but their answers, whatever they may be. Use the words, "What do you think...?" so they know you are looking for opinions. If needed, set some rules for your discussion: if the group is rowdy, maybe they have to hold your stuffed animal before they can speak. Don't let silence intimidate you, and resist the temptation to give the answers away too soon. If there are other groups having discussions nearby, show a little respect by keeping your campers at a reasonable energy level until everyone is done.

The setting and physical arrangement of your discussion group are very important. Campers in a row on a fence with their leader standing in front of them and a lawnmower roaring in the background is not an arrangement that lends itself to discussion. Neither is allowing campers to lie on their bunks while you pace the room and try to keep them awake. Sit in a tight circle or in a corner of the room where everyone can see each other and distractions are limited—a blanket can create a defined space for this. Or pile everyone onto your bunk! If you can, find a suitable place outside for your discussion (with appropriate permission). I remember a night on a canoe trip, camped out under an incredible array of stars. No lights anywhere, not even a moon. After singing together, we all laid on our backs looking up at the brilliant night sky to pray. No one prayed—out loud anyway—and we watched for fifteen minutes not speaking a word. Many of the teens said it was one of the most significant experiences of their lives. One of them said it was the first time he had taken God seriously, and not long after this, he came to faith in Christ. And no one had said a thing—except the stars.

With some groups, leading discussions will be the hardest thing you do all day. Some kids cannot sit still and listen for very long; give them a positive distraction, like paper to doodle or a small exercise ball to squeeze. Some campers will monopolize the discussion; others won't say a thing. Gently direct your more interesting questions to the quieter camper, and encourage campers to respectfully respond to one another's opinions. Rather than think you have to fill the time, let the discussion run its course and then move on to talking about other things. You want campers to look forward to these times, not simply get them over with. Keep in mind that God is on your side in this challenge, and enter discussions with prayer and anticipation of what he will do.

Think about this:
- I encourage you to try out building discussion sandwiches a few times before you go to camp. Maybe you could lead a discussion in your youth group or with friends.

Here is a short list of activities, ideas and questions to use for the bottom or top bun of your discussion sandwich. Bon appetit!

- Invite another staff member to visit your cabin dressed a certain way or to help with a skit.
- Run a scenario: have campers act out what they would do about a situation.
- Read them a suitable children's book that you brought with you.
- Play charades or *Pictionary* using words related to your passage.
- Have them ask twenty yes or no questions to guess a character, object or animal.
- Do a scavenger hunt for objects that describe your idea.
- "Ten years from now…" Have them make some predictions about themselves.
- Theater sports—use classic drama class activities to introduce your idea.
- Make up a song or commercial about an idea.
- What is the hardest thing about being your age?
- What superpower would you most want to have?
- What I liked best about today was…
- To make life better I would invent…
- What would you do with three wishes?
- If Jesus was sitting in our circle, what would you ask him?

8. Listen to Campers' Problems

Do you remember the story of the Good Samaritan (Luke 10:25-37)? A Jewish guy is on the hazardous road from Jerusalem to Jericho when the worst happens—he is mugged, beaten and left for dead. No one stops to help except a Samaritan, a mixed race despised by the Jews. His willingness to get involved has become the embodiment of compassion and can be a model for people-helping in the camp community.

In the secure setting of camp, it is likely some of your campers will confide in you concerning their personal and family problems. They may have questions that have gone unanswered for years. When children or youth show this kind of trust and confidence in you, it is a compliment, and it was probably not easy for them to do. The camp leader must be ready to take up the role of "people-helper" when individual campers come to talk. What qualifies you to do this? They came to you. What are you qualified to do? Mostly just listen with care and understanding, and if needed refer them to a more qualified caregiver.

That is what the Good Samaritan did. Simply stopping to help was a risk that several others in the story had thought too great. When you stop what you are doing to help a camper, there are risks involved. What they tell you may be painful to hear, even traumatic. You may feel helpless, and you may make mistakes. Most of all, you will need to act on what they tell you, which could be anything from praying with them to reporting an adult to the authorities. Follow-up after their week at camp may be necessary. The risk may cause you to hesitate, but I hope you will follow the Samaritan's example and approach the camper to offer your time, your love and your help.

You can imagine that the first questions the Good Samaritan asked the man in the ditch were, "Are you okay?" and "What happened?" and that he listened intently to the man's mumbled reply as he poured wine and olive oil on his wounds. I am not sure what the first aid attendant at your camp would say about these methods, but you have wine and oil at your disposal in a spiritual sense. The wine was for cleansing and disinfecting; when a camper comes to you, the wine will be your ability to listen and respond so they will talk more. While they talk, emotion is released, fears and loneliness are relieved, anger is vented. Cleansing takes place. Be real but careful as you express your own emotional response; ask the camper questions for clarification, and briefly say back to the camper what you are hearing. When the dirt is washed away, you may expose some very raw wounds. The olive oil soothes and relieves pain; it is your compassion and understanding that will do that spiritually, and your prayers will bandage the place that hurts. All of this talking has enabled the camper to see their situation more objectively, and now someone who cares, knows.

The fact that you know their situation could elevate their fears again, and you should assure confidentiality, with conditions. It may be necessary for you to pass on what you have heard to another person for the camper's protection or healing. If the conversation begins with, "Don't tell anyone, but…" you will need to assure them you will not tell anyone unless you need to find additional help, and you will only talk with the person who can offer that help. Hopefully, they will still trust you enough to continue the conversation. Be careful not to give specifics to any other staff; for example, at a staff meeting simply ask prayer for that camper without going into detail. Choose an appropriate location for your one-on-one conversation with the camper: in a public place, but far enough away that the camper feels free to talk. Whenever you can, read with the camper what the word of God says about their issue, wielding the Bible as a fine instrument, not a clumsy sword. Always, always offer to pray with a camper about their situation.

The Samaritan realized this man would require longer and better care than he could provide on the road, so he put him on his donkey and took him to the equivalent of a hospital: a roadside inn. Very often, your conversation with a camper is all they will need from you, but some situations may require long-term and even professional help. How will you know? There are some issues that should always be immediately referred to your direct supervisor at camp, who will manage any consequent decisions and actions. These include: any threat of suicide; a disclosure of physical, sexual or other abuse; a verbal threat of violence against another person; severe or unusual behavior; and any other situation that may pose a danger to the camper or other people. There are other situations that may require referral to your supervisor, who will likely only contact the parents: evidence of anorexia or bulimia; evidence or disclosure of self-injury such as cutting, burning or embedding; severe depression; disclosure of drug or alcohol abuse. In addition, you should seek the advice of the appropriate camp leader any time the situation is very uncomfortable for you or beyond your ability to respond. This is not failure on your part; it is the right thing to do in the best interest of the camper.

Finally, the Samaritan made a promise to check up on the patient and make sure all was well with him. If you have referred a camper to another helper, it doesn't relieve you of responsibility. Your continued care and interest—and your prayers—will still mean much to the camper. If possible and appropriate, offer to call or visit the camper after the week; if that is not possible, at least check with your supervisor to see if there is any update, and hopefully, you can send a note of interest and encouragement. If parents are part of the problem, be careful not to side against a parent or give advice that might be misconstrued. If your camp or the camper's parents ask you not to communicate with the camper, back off and keep on praying. There may be times you will wish the camper could just stay with you forever, especially when you realize the tears on the last day are not only because she is saying goodbye to you. Do what you reasonably can, and pray to the God who sees the sparrow fall.

There are many kinds of issues you may confront at camp, and hopefully, resources and advice will be available to you there. The following list of common problems may help you listen to campers with better care and understanding, and know when to seek further help for them.

The majority of issues brought to you will have to do with **relationships**: conflict between friends; pressure or harassment from bullies; parent and family problems; fallout from sexual relationships; an inability to forgive a wrong. These issues will sometimes resolve themselves as campers talk, but it is possible referral will be necessary, especially if there is any physical or emotional threat to the camper. You have the best of resources for relational problems—the Bible says to "forgive as the Lord forgave you" (Col 3:13), and many relational issues have to do with an inability or unwillingness to forgive someone. A good starting place is to tell them about a God who does not treat us as our sins deserve (mercy) and does good toward us that we can't earn (grace).

Tragic circumstances sometimes follow kids to camp. The loss of a loved one, a sudden move to a new town or some other crisis may be a recent occurrence and still quite emotionally raw, seeping with anger, mourning, even guilt. Parents may be correct that camp is a safe place for kids to recover, but usually what hurting kids want is home, family and normalcy. If that isn't possible, a grieving camper will require large amounts of your time as a camp leader. You may also feel a bit helpless, as there is nothing you can do but be there for them, listen when they want to talk and, almost always, bite your tongue when tempted to say words you think might be comforting. Be assured you are not doing nothing— your presence with the camper is the most appreciated gift you could offer anyone. It will also be very draining, so talk with the camp admin to see if other staff can relieve you so you can rest and give attention to your other campers. The hurting camper can also be encouraged—but not coerced—to get involved in the camp activities to give relief to their fixation on the object of their pain. But expect they will have little interest in things that seem so trivial in comparison. Your follow-up with a camper facing grief will be greatly appreciated.

Homesickness is a specific type of grief, a sense of temporary loss that can be nearly as intense as permanent loss. The signs to watch for are tears, lack of enthusiasm, isolation and stress indicators such as stomach-aches, as any grieving child might experience. If the distraction of camp activities is not enough, conversation about home can be surprisingly helpful—ask questions about their family, pets, interests, fun memories and what they plan to do when they return home. Let them know their feelings are normal and help them with short-term goals (for example, waiting until Wednesday to phone home). Involve them in activities they enjoy the most and connect them with other staff, such as a camp grandma and grandpa or camp pastor. If they do need to go home, don't give them the impression that they have failed or that you are disappointed; talk about "next summer."

For some campers, **basic insecurities** are magnified in the unfamiliar setting of camp. They become ultra-shy or do not attempt activities for fear of failure or ridicule. They may become very self-conscious about their bodies, having never before shared a bedroom or showered in a public washroom. It is unlikely an insecure camper will easily confide in you, but if you notice the signs of insecurity there are things you can do to increase their confidence. Help them choose activities in which they can excel; avoid leaving that camper alone in the cabin with the other campers; be approachable and build trust; share the Gospel of grace and forgiveness. Severe insecurity can become **depression**, as self-conscious fears turn into despair and hopelessness. Care and understanding will be appreciated, but your well-intended advice might lead to greater misery. The severely depressed camper will need referral to long-term help.

Discipleship includes dealing with **sin and habitual problems**, which God often confronts in the setting of camp. Your goal is confession, which means the camper sees her sin as God sees it and is ready to turn her back on that way of life. Sin is sin; take it seriously any time a camper wants to talk about these problems, even if you think they are not significant. Gently help him understand God's viewpoint on his actions or thoughts, not in a condemning way, but so he comes into agreement with God. Serious problems—addiction to pornography, drug or alcohol abuse, confession to crime or abuse of others—may require long-term solutions, so referral to your supervisor or at least some kind of accountability will be necessary. Dealing with sin is another great opportunity to talk about the forgiveness available in the Gospel; assure the believing camper of the promise that God is "faithful and just and will forgive us our sins and purify us from all unrighteousness" (1 John 1:9).

Any disclosure of **abuse** must be taken very seriously, whether physical, sexual or emotional abuse, or neglect. The unwritten rules in the world of the abused are: don't talk; don't trust; don't feel. When a child or teen breaks these rules and tells you what they have experienced, it is like attempting to escape from prison. They may not tell you openly; they may instead drop hints, start conversations about things a child shouldn't know, or simply not hide the bruises on their body. There is injustice here; someone is taking advantage of their power over the child, and you have the opportunity to tip the balance of power in the camper's favor. Don't miss it! Reasonable suspicion of abuse *must* be reported to the appropriate leader at your camp. You may be asked some very basic questions about what the camper told you, but you do not need to press the camper for details. Encourage the camper to express the emotions surrounding the abuse, and respond with understanding, affirmation and love. This experience may also be traumatic for you and require your own conversation with a caregiver.

Bullying is a form of abuse that takes place among peers. We will discuss how to deal with bullying that takes place at camp, but a camper might have the courage to tell you about intimidation taking place at school or their neighborhood or online. Bullying is not just physical these days; more commonly, bullies use emotional abuse, shunning, shaming and destruction of image and reputation, both in person and online. Cyber-bullying is especially innovative and cruel, and its forms are almost without limit: everything from re-posting private information or photos, to threats and blackmail. As with other forms of abuse, the traumatic effects of bullying go far beyond the actual event, especially if the camper lives under the fear it may happen again. This can produce dangerous levels of hopelessness and despair, and may lead to other problems such as depression, substance abuse and self-injury. Depending on the severity of the problem, intervention will likely be necessary in the form of talking with your supervisor, which usually results in a conversation with the camper's parents. Surprisingly, many parents do not take bullying seriously enough until it is too late, as shown by recent incidents of teen suicide. Even if the camper no longer needs intervention, you can affirm the injustice of the situation, deal with forgiveness and give them ideas and tools to avoid it happening again. When you listen with care and understanding to their story, you promote cleansing and healing of wounds and tip the balance of power in the camper's favor.

Self-injury is a plague that occasionally becomes endemic, especially among teen girls. It is important to understand that most self-injurers are not attempting to end their life; rather, they rely on their practices for survival (see *Hope and Healing for Kids*

Who Cut, Marv Penner, 2008). Self-injury is damaging and dangerous, both physically and emotionally, and is very addictive. Practices include making incisions through the skin with a razor blade, writing words deeply into the skin with pens or needles, burning the skin and embedding objects under the skin to induce pain whenever they feel it is needed. These practices allow them to act out their feelings against themselves and also release endorphins to give temporary relief to emotional pain. Self-injury can be the drug of choice for nice church kids who would never turn to narcotics or alcohol to deal with their emotional pain and think they can keep this one hidden and under control. Long-term care and accountability are necessary, and if you are the only one they will ever tell it may need to be you. If so, seek counsel and resources, and if the self-injury is severe enough to require a trip to the doctor you should refer the camper to your supervisor, or if camp is over, to the parent. Your goal is to help the camper go longer and longer between episodes and to receive each setback with love, grace and the encouragement to try again.

Family break-up is prevalent, more so every year. The divorce rate is increasing even though more and more couples never get married, and the break-up rate of unmarried couples is much higher than that of married couples. It would not be unusual to have more campers in a cabin with single or stepparents than those who have both birth parents at home. You might think that as a society our families would have learned to tolerate this instability by now; however, the trauma of family break-up is severe in practically every case and is usually most suffered by the children. They are often hurting and angry kids, struggling with strong emotions children shouldn't have to face, such as anger and hatred, shame and embarrassment, rejection, depression, guilt (from being told or assuming it was their fault), hostility, aggression and confusion. These emotions are often suppressed and may show themselves in unexpected outbursts and rebellious behavior in otherwise nice kids. Again, you may feel helpless but you have much to offer these campers. Be firm but compassionate in your discipline, and lend them your understanding and caring ears. They may have no one else to talk with about their family and how they feel.

There may also be times when *you* need to talk with someone who will listen with love and understanding. Even in a week, exhaustion can rob you of creativity and motivation, and a half-hour one-on-one with your head cabin leader might be better than a nap. Perhaps you are the target of strong temptations. Get over the embarrassment of talking with a camp pastor or leader, rather than embarrass your whole camp with moral failure. You might have doubts and questions that limit your effectiveness as a spiritual leader or conflicts with another staff member that limit you both. You may have come to camp with problems like the ones we have just discussed and feel disqualified to offer support to campers. Don't be afraid to avail yourself of the advisors God has placed around you for the week. They want you healthy in body and soul, so go to your leaders before your hesitation turns to regret.

Think about this:

- What resources do you have in books, people and experience that can prepare you to be a people-helper at camp?
- What personal issues should you take to a trusted caregiver before you arrive at camp?
- Who has been (or can be) a mentor to you—someone with more maturity and experience who connects with you regularly and whose example you are following?

9. Manage Discipline Issues

This is the chapter you hope you will never use. Who wants to discipline kids at a fun place like camp? Stay with me, though, because I want you to notice that the word "discipline" looks very much like the word "disciple." Discipline is not simply punishing kids for bad behavior, and punishment without discipline is child abuse. Rather, discipline is teaching campers how to live rightly and have better relationships with people, so it is very closely related to discipleship and teaching them to follow Jesus. Let me take it further: discipline should result in a better week for your camper than she would have had if you had failed to discipline her. Even further: discipline should result in a better relationship with her than you had before, because you cared enough to confront and deal with an issue fairly and wisely.

Remember the blind guy whose furniture you moved around? Campers arrive at camp and find that all the rules and boundaries are in unfamiliar places, and there are new ones they have never seen before. They will likely trip up at some point and will need correction. A camp leader has no right to employ disagreeable consequences for a camper's behavior apart from the loving purpose of teaching him right living and improving his relationships with people. Discipline is not pursuing justice but grace.

Effective discipline of your campers takes a careful balance of two things: love and control, or you could say nurture and boundaries. The balance between these two can be ordered into four distinctive styles of discipline:

Severe—All control, no love. In this style of discipline, campers are not getting their own way, but they also do not feel loved by their leader. There is an absence of warmth and laughter in the cabin; an outward appearance of order is all that matters to the cabin leader. Campers tend to become afraid or rebellious. This style of discipline is the least effective in training campers to live rightly. Studies show that in the home setting, a severe discipline style results in low self-esteem, rebellion and rejection of the parent's beliefs.

Neglect—No control, no love. Campers get their own way because of an absence of care. Though slightly better than the style above, this one creates emotional distance between campers and their leader, who is often simply absent. The leader might return with sudden attempts at control or kindness that fail because of the lack of consistency and respect. Kids can read when someone has no interest in them; they feel rejected, and look for care elsewhere.

Permissive—No control, lots of love. Campers get their own way, but at least they know they are valued. This is a risky style of discipline; however, it is second best and better than exercising too much control. The cabin leader may be seeking the approval of the campers because of personal insecurities. There is no doubt the leader loves them, but kids will keep pushing for all they can get. Unfortunately, there is probably little true respect for the cabin leader, and spiritual instruction may be less effective because the leader's words have little impact on the daily behavior of the campers.

Healthy—Control with love. Campers do not get their own way because their leader is looking out for their best interest. There is a nurturing environment of involvement, interaction and open communication. Kids feel secure in the fair boundaries the leader has established, and are excited about the direction the leader is taking them. If you think about it, this is God's style of discipline, as the writer of Hebrews tells us: "God disciplines us for our good, in order that we may share in his holiness" (Heb 12:10). Campers usually respond with respect, compliance and a desire to become like their leader. It matches the servant-leadership style of Jesus and is all about discipleship.

Because discipline is about learning, prevention is a big part of it—you don't need to wait until problems develop. The better you know your campers, the more you will catch issues before they become a problem. For example, some kids are bullied because they are intentionally annoying, so deal with the irritation before you have to deal with bullying as well. Let campers know the boundaries so they don't stumble over them. Perhaps the camp director goes over the guidelines with everyone on the first day, but who is listening in all the excitement? Go over the rules again that first evening, framing it with, "I really want all of us to have a great week." Be around your campers in those in-between times when there is not much going on and problems are most likely to show up. Avoid letting your campers get overtired, which will lead to bad attitudes and flaring tempers. Praise their good behavior. Give that "bad apple" you were warned about a fresh start and the opportunity to have a different experience than last summer.

When it is time to confront a problem with a camper, seek to understand before entertaining accusations or announcing consequences. Rather than enter the situation with, "That's it, you are all in big trouble!" start with, "Is everyone okay? Tell me what happened here." If safety is not an issue, take your time to evaluate the situation, and avoid escalating the problem through verbal exchange. Appropriate consequences for a camper's bad behavior are pretty limited, and often the natural consequences are enough. You might give a "time out" to cool tempers or redirect energy by getting them to clean up a mess they made, but there are not many other penalties you can require of a camper that would be considered appropriate by a reasonable parent, which is your rule of thumb. Often your best option is to talk it through with a camper, which is also a great opportunity for further discipleship. You want to help them see the problem as you see it, as well as how those who were affected see it and as God sees it. Decide together how to set it right again. For example, you can show them that trust was broken in the cabin when they helped themselves to other campers' stuff, and that respect needs to be re-established.

Punishment that fails to have the positive learning aspects of discipline is clearly not appropriate. Any form of physical punishment is not only inappropriate but likely illegal: you cannot handle a camper roughly, shake him, hit him, or take almost any other physical action. It is also inappropriate to force him to do things that are physically demanding or threatening, such as running up and down stairs, doing push-ups until exhausted or staying out in the rain. Verbal or emotional attack (for example, shouting, shaming, guilting or shunning) is abuse, not discipline. Many kids face put-downs and yelling every day at home; don't let that become part of their camp experience. Be aware of your motives when deciding on consequences—favoritism or retaliation have no place in teaching campers better behavior.

Always wrap up discipline with an affirmation of your love and acceptance; forgive and put the matter behind you. Let them know their slate is clean. Kids will not always respond well to discipline. Even if they remain sullen and resentful, you must affirm you love them, though you disapprove of their attitude and behavior. Again, as much as it is up to you, discipline should result in a better relationship with your campers.

Here are some of the issues that may require discipline this summer and some suggestions on managing them:

Dishonesty is usually an attempt to regain control in a situation where we have lost it. For example, a camper is afraid he will not be accepted by his fellow campers, so he invents or exaggerates a story about some amazing thing he did. People cheat in games to gain the upper hand; often their reason for stealing is simply that someone has something they don't have. Because dishonesty is usually self-focused, the goal of discipline is to help the camper to realize the feelings, rights and needs of others, and become one who seeks to share instead of one who takes (Eph 4:28). This change of heart in the camper will hopefully change their behavior. The most difficult part of dealing with dishonesty is getting at the truth, especially when accusations start flying. Ask God for clarification, talk individually with those involved, get advice as needed, have guilty campers make things right and seek peace in your cabin.

Intimidation and harm of people is also a control issue. One camper or a group of campers uses whatever leverage they have—strength, aggression, numbers, social media, secrets—to gain power over another. Because of the potential damage to bodies and emotions, prevention is the best method of dealing with bullies and scrappers. Be aware of rising tensions and don't hesitate to step in and deal with them before harm is done. Avoid leaving your campers by themselves in the cabin or other places out of view where taunting can quickly escalate into aggression. Let campers know you welcome them to talk with you about anything that makes them feel uncomfortable during the week, and promote an atmosphere of acceptance and loyalty in your group. If bullying or physical harm takes place, immediate intervention and action are needed, and your supervisor should be brought into the situation right away. Gone are the days of, "Let them work it out themselves." In addition to the actual physical, emotion and social harm that is done, children and youth who suffer under bullies experience significant stress and trauma and are much more likely to wrestle with depression and thoughts of suicide. Take every report or suspicion seriously, and tip the balance of power in favor of the oppressed.

Disturbance problems might include talking or bothering other people at chapels or firesides, or starting a food fight at a meal. Prevention is possible and is your best way of maintaining discipline. Watch where your campers sit at a meeting (if they are not with you) and place yourself in the middle of the hotspot, even if it means rearranging the seating in a friendly way. Redirect potentially disturbing energy at the table into fun stuff—like contests to see who is going to scrape the plates—so that, as with all discipline, the result is a better relationship with your campers. When confronting disturbances—such as a group of campers running wild after the night game —keep in mind that the goal is to calm down the situation and return emotions to normal, so be careful not to escalate the situation by yelling or chasing down campers.

Problems of the tongue, says the book of James, have the potential to do great damage and quickly spread harm (James 3:1-12). Swearing might include obscenity (socially unacceptable words), profanity (improper use of God's name) and cursing (verbal aggression or abuse). Inappropriate stories or jokes are in the same category. As guests in our space, campers must uphold the house rules. Don't ignore swearing, but tell campers why it is inappropriate and keep on top of occurrences to help them stop. Watch for other destructive use of words such as gossip, shaming and cutting remarks. Again, do not let them continue or these problems will inevitably escalate like a spark in a dry bush. Get advice and support from your supervisor if the problem does not immediately stop. Set this as the standard for your campers: "Do not let any unwholesome talk come out of your mouths, but only what is helpful for building others up according to their needs, that it may benefit those who listen" (Eph 4:29).

Problems of the heart are harder to identify and to discipline because they have to do with attitude more than action. You might have a camper who is uncooperative and defensive and not know why. Another might bring into the cabin an attitude of criticism, prejudice, disrespect or hostility against those who are not like him. On the other end of the scale, there might be complacency and apathy where you would rather see involvement or spiritual progress. You may be tempted to react when these negative attitudes show themselves, even though they likely have nothing to do with you. Remember how little you know about your campers and respond instead with a desire to understand the source of these attitudes and a determination and patience to see them change.

For some campers, extreme attitudes and actions may be a sign of a **behavioral disorder**. Attention Deficit Hyperactivity Disorder (ADHD) can cause constant restlessness, an inability to focus on what is happening or said to them, and impulsive behavior. You should not assume a camper has ADHD unless this is confirmed by the camper's medical form, but if the attitude or behavior is very abnormal the camp medical staff are your first advisors. Usually, an ADHD camper is on very strong medication, but some parents will use camp as a break from the meds —which may be recommended by a doctor but is tough for the cabin leader! An ADHD child will likely have difficulty with the intense social environment of camp and will require supervision, structure and downtime. Love the camper and do what is needed to protect him and those around him, but don't expect much progress in disciplining his behavior. May compassion overcome frustration.

Damage or destruction of personal or camp property is possible. You should not have in your cabin any item you can't afford to lose, and neither should your campers. Usually, camps have a policy that will help you prevent problems with campers' expensive items such as electronic devices and jewelry, but occasionally a parent will insist a camper carry their cell phone at all times. You will usually need to refer an issue of damaged property to your supervisor, as parents may need to get involved to pay for damages. You can handle the discipline side of things by actually dealing with the issue rather than letting it go, and having a conversation about doing toward others what we would have them do toward us (Matt 7:12). Most camps no longer permit the old-school "raids" where one cabin pranks another, but damage can be caused by practical jokes that go too far. Redirect any talk about pranking into more constructive plans; secret acts of kindness are just as fun.

For older campers who come from a world of sexual encouragement, **guy/girl issues** are likely. Your camp will have policies about "public displays of affection" but there are no policies more awkward to enforce than these. Prevention—in the form of frank talks about what is acceptable and what is not— will be your best discipline, but you may have to confront a couple who is acting inappropriately, either in terms of their physical touch or social exclusion of others. If possible, bring along the cabin leader of the opposite sex to deal with the problem, and always take the campers away from the crowd—yet in a public place—to talk with them. Often it will be best to talk with the campers individually rather than as a couple. Remember that the moral boundaries at camp are set in places campers are not used to, so this is an opportunity to teach. If there is no change or if the situation is becoming serious, bring your supervisor into the picture.

Until the last number of years, camps thought sexual problems could be avoided by keeping the guys out of the girls' cabin area. But **same-sex liaisons** are also an issue that should not be ignored and are particularly difficult to discipline in the camp setting without accusations of homophobia. There should be no difference between the way camp leaders deal with inappropriate same-sex behavior and the way they deal with lines crossed heterosexually. There is no place for sexual activity, displays, conversation, or intimidation in any camp setting, no matter the age of the campers. At the same time, cabin leaders should protect campers from bullying that is related to sexual orientation, or perceived sexual orientation. Some kids are labeled "gay" for erroneous reasons, such as personality or interests. This is far too weighted an issue in our day to allow it to be the subject of jokes or ridicule.

Social acceptance of **recreational drugs and alcohol**—even among believers—is making it harder to talk with campers about the issue. In any case, these substances obviously have no place at a summer camp, even for staff, and will need to be reported and taken away. Camps vary in their response to catching campers smoking or with other prohibited substances, but even if it means someone will have to go home you will not help the camper or your camp if you let them get away with it. Rather than argue with the camper's rationalizations, focus your conversation around the principles of God's word: "'I have the right to do anything,' you say—but not everything is beneficial. 'I have the right to do anything'—but I will not be mastered by anything" (1 Cor 6:12). Be aware your example is being watched, listened to and followed by campers. During and after camp, even if your conscience allows you to use these substances, don't be guilty of causing a camper to stumble because of your words or actions (Rom 14:19-21).

Can you really grow your relationship with a camper through discipline? Absolutely! Is that not how God deals with you: revealing what he expects of you, confronting you when you mess up, lovingly correcting your behavior—over and over again to train you to live righteously (see 2 Tim 3:16-17)? With this in mind, you might not cringe when your campers start accusing one another about the missing chocolate bar—it is just another opportunity for mercy and grace. It is all discipleship.

Think about this:
- What is the style of discipline with which you are most familiar?

How might you best respond to some of these situations?
- A camper won't participate in games and activities and never wants to leave your side.
- One of your campers often lashes out in anger toward other campers for no apparent reason.
- A camper refuses to go to chapel or anything else that has to do with God.
- Several valuable items have gone missing from your cabin, including some of your own.
- You discover that an older camper has been telling stories about sex to other campers when you are not around.
- All the campers in your cabin are from Christian homes, except one who swears like a sailor.
- You suspect that one of your campers is bullying and intimidating several others when you are not around, but there is no hard evidence.
- Your camper complains to you that his camera has been stolen, and he accuses another camper in the cabin of taking it.

10. Make Disciples

"Always be prepared to give an answer to everyone who asks you to give the reason for the hope that you have. But do this with gentleness and respect" (1 Peter 3:15-16).

It is a little bit like Peter telling us to always be ready with our chainsaw. The Gospel is a very powerful tool (see Rom 1:16), capable of eternal good or great damage, depending in part on how it is wielded. That is why Peter says to temper it with gentleness and respect. Gentleness is power under control, like a bodybuilder dad with a newborn baby. Respect is taking people from where they are and moving them toward Jesus with care. We could threaten campers that they are going to hell apart from Jesus, because it is true. But you do not want them to respond as one little girl did when her mom arrived to pick her up at the end of the week of camp. She gave her a big hug and said, "Guess what, mom?

You're going to hell!" That is a situation of power out of control; the girl should have been instructed in more prudent ways of handling this sword.

The evangelist Paul understood the urgency to do this well: "Devote yourselves to prayer, being watchful and thankful. And pray for us, too, that God may open a door for our message, so that we may proclaim the mystery of Christ, for which I am in chains. Pray that I may proclaim it clearly, as I should. Be wise in the way you act toward outsiders; make the most of every opportunity. Let your conversation be always full of grace, seasoned with salt, so that you may know how to answer everyone" (Col 4:2-6). Notice he doesn't say, "Study hard so you can get this Gospel thing right." He says we should pray, and then live in such a way that when the opportunity comes we will have the right answer to give.

Can you grow tomatoes? Ah, trick question—you can't! Earlier, we discussed Paul pointing out that all we can do is provide the right environment for things to grow. A seed, the Gospel, is planted in the soil of a camper's heart; we apply water, fertilizer, sunlight and careful weeding—all these optimal conditions for growth—and just watch what happens! We can say we have made a disciple of Jesus, but really God did the growing. We simply cooperated.

As mentioned before, the camp community offers great conditions for spiritual growth—relationships, the Gospel, creation, crisis, hospitality, prayer, miracles. Here are a few more ways you can work cooperatively with God to bring campers into his kingdom:

Take your time. There is no need to pressure a

camper. God is patient with us, not wanting anyone to perish, but everyone to come to repentance (2 Peter 3:9). You will not help your tomato plant grow by pulling on its branches. It takes a long time for a butterfly to emerge from its cocoon, and if you try to speed things up it will die. You may feel the urgency of having so few days with a camper, but your role might only be to plant a seed or water it, and someone else will bring it to harvest.

Share your life. Remember Paul's example of ministry? "We were delighted to share with you not only the gospel of God but our lives as well" (1 Thes 2:8). He didn't just spin a message; he did life with those he was hoping to reach. He knew they would make decisions about him long before they made a decision about the Jesus he followed. Your campers need to see Jesus in the very ordinary parts of daily camp life, from brushing your teeth in the morning to the stories you share from your past as you paddle across the lake.

Be generous. There are two things the world values the most: time and money. When you are generous with both, the people of the world take notice. In Luke 16, Jesus told a parable to teach us to be shrewd in our use of resources, wasting them on the kingdom of God. Look for opportunities to be fully available to your campers, with nothing distracting your attention. Take up this challenge: buy nothing for yourself from the camp store all week; only buy stuff for other people to open up opportunities for conversation.

Speak Jesus. You could work hard at creating a fine garden, but it would not be much good if you never planted anything. "How, then, can they call on the one they have not believed in? And how can they believe in the one of whom they have not heard?" (Rom 10:14). You hope your campers will put their faith in Jesus, so it is important to talk about him— the stories of his life, work and teaching—so they get to know him.

Don't quench the Spirit's fire; let him do what only he can do. "No one can come to me unless the Father who sent me draws them," said Jesus (John 6:44). I find more and more that my definition of ministry is simply to get out of God's way so he can work. You will make mistakes during your week of camp; set them right by apologizing to campers. Keep their eternal interests ahead of your temporal ones.

Expect to win. Jesus said the gates of hell would not prevail against the church (Matt 16:17-19). I used to picture the church in a defensive stance, fighting off the attack of hell. Look more carefully. It is the realm of the dead that is under attack, and Jesus promises it will not withstand the siege of the church. That is what will happen this summer. You, along with all of us, will crash the gates of hell and rescue campers who have lived there all their lives! Nothing will stop us when we move in Jesus' name. Even in campers' hearts where there is no apparent progress, God's purposes move forward. Again, be faithful and leave the results to God.

When you pray and live this way before campers, the Holy Spirit stirs in their hearts. They have seen in you a different way to think and live and will begin to wonder why. They may ask you "the reason for the hope that you have," or some other question that displays an open heart. How will you respond? Is this the place where you lack confidence: knowing what to say when presented with an opportunity to explain the Gospel?

There are several reasons for your apprehension. First, there is an element of mystery to the Gospel. In response to Nicodemus' question of how a person is born again, Jesus said, "The wind blows wherever it pleases. You hear its sound, but you cannot tell where it comes from or where it is going. So it is with everyone born of the Spirit" (John 3:8). Each person's journey toward Jesus is unique, and the means by which they come to faith is not a formula or package. I cannot give you four things to tell them that will bring them into the kingdom of God.

In addition, there are several traditional phrases— most of them not found in the Bible—that have muddied the waters of the Gospel message. It may surprise you to learn that the most common of these —"ask Jesus into your heart"—is a human invention. It probably came from Jesus' invitation in Rev 3:20 to open the door and let him in, but in that passage it was the church, not the unbeliever, that was ignoring his knock. The phrase says nothing about sin and repentance, faith and forgiveness. A camper might ask Jesus into her heart like she invites a friend to a slumber party, or set Jesus on a shelf along with his collection of household gods. Amazingly, kids still come to genuine faith in Jesus by this route, but it is due to God's faithfulness despite our carelessness.

We also commonly talk about "accepting Jesus as Lord and Savior." Again, there is little support for the phrase in the New Testament. The word "accept" or "receive" in John 1:11-12 means that people welcomed Jesus' message, not that they somehow acquired Jesus himself. More importantly, once they welcomed his message they "believed in his name," and that is how they became children of God. There is also a popular idea that a person can receive Jesus as Savior and at a later point accept him as Lord. Jesus did not seem interested in attracting this kind of follower (Luke 9:57-62). He is not an option that we might choose among many alternatives; rather, we are all in rebellion against God, who graciously accepts those who surrender and put their faith in Jesus.

Why does it seem so difficult to articulate what a person needs to hear and what they have to do to become a Christian? It can't be that hard—remember Jesus' prayer, "I praise you, Father, Lord of heaven and earth, because you have hidden these things from the wise and learned, and revealed them to little children." (Matt 11:25-26). Paul affirms this when he talks about the "foolishness" of the message of the cross that shames the wise (1 Cor 1:18-31). Perhaps in our attempts to simplify or package the message—especially for children—we have made it more unfathomable than ever.

What is the Gospel?

The first verse of Mark says, "The beginning of the gospel of Jesus the Messiah, the Son of God…" The word "gospel" is from the archaic "good spell," which means good news or story or message. Mark's use of the word "Messiah" gives historical roots to his message—the promise of a coming Messiah is found throughout the Old Testament. What follows is Mark's careful account of the life, work, teaching, suffering, death and resurrection of Jesus, given without interpretation. The writings of Paul, Peter, John and others that complete the New Testament explain what the good story means. So in a sense, you could say the entire Bible is the Gospel, the unfolding of God's purposes in the person of Jesus the Messiah.

When Jesus went around proclaiming the Gospel, he announced the fulfillment of the prophecies and the arrival of the kingdom of God (Mark 1:14-15). He also called his people to repent and believe this good news, and they were baptized as the sign of their faith. The message did not change after his death and resurrection; Peter told his convicted crowd of listeners, "Repent and be baptized, every one of you, in the name of Jesus Christ for the forgiveness of your sins" (Acts 2:38). The Gospel is the revelation of Jesus as the Messiah, and the right response to the Gospel is repentance and faith, affirmed through baptism.

Too tough for eight-year-olds? My experience is that kids love the stories about Jesus, who told his disciples to allow the children to crawl up on his lap. Perhaps it seems too easy: that they could believe in Jesus and experience a change in their trajectory, from a life of serving sin and self to one of following the Savior. Surely they are too young to be baptized! But it all happened to me at this age, and I am forever grateful.

Here is how we make it tough for eight-year-olds: for some reason, we find it necessary to seal the deal. There is a prayer they have to pray, or we make them stand up at fireside or come forward at chapel, or they sign the little statement in the back of their Gideon

Bible. That way we can ensure the transaction happened and they are now saved. We count them up and make a report at the end of the summer of all our conversions, and we feel good about it. But there is no instruction or example in the New Testament of someone becoming a believer by praying a prayer, raising their hand in a meeting or signing a response card. How many campers end up doing these actions over and over again, afraid they didn't do it right the first time, or wondering if they really meant it?

People become believers in Jesus by believing in Jesus. How simple is that? A child comes to you and says she wants to become a Christian like you. So you tell her (or remind her) about Jesus, what he did and taught and how he died to take away our sin and came to life again. You talk about your own faith in Jesus, how you left your old way of life behind to follow him, and why it is hard and why it is good. And you ask her if that is what she wants for herself, and she says yes. Then you give her a big hug and tell her you are so happy for her. Probably you will pray for her, and she might want to talk with Jesus too but it is okay if she doesn't. Maybe that night you encourage her to tell the cabin group about her new faith in Jesus. And the rest of the week you teach her how to pray, get her started in her Bible, tell her about what you do when you are tempted or mess up, and discuss the details of helping her attend the nearby church of a friend of yours. It ain't rocket science. If you think that is too simple, compare Philip's conversation with the Ethiopian man: "Then Philip opened his mouth, and beginning with this Scripture he told him the good news about Jesus" (Acts 8:35). The Holy Spirit does all the real work in her heart;

remember, your job is to cooperate.

How do you feel about sharing your faith now?

I want to underline what I said earlier about "gentleness and respect." Think of the power of persuasion you have over a camper: you are an adult who actually wants to spend time with him; you maybe go to chapels together to hear a professional speaker and a pretty good worship band; you are watching your camper's response at an emotionally-charged fireside; even their friends are talking about God; and then they want to talk with you about faith in Christ. You could so easily manipulate him into the kingdom of God. And that would be wrong. Jesus didn't use soft music and starry nights to woo disciples; he often said things that made it difficult for people to follow him. Paul said he preached the Gospel with pure motives, not with trickery or flattery or deception (1 Thes 2:3-7). If emotions are running too high, wait. The last thing you want is a camper who the next day feels that in a moment of weakness he was conned into a decision he now regrets.

Respect wherever a camper is coming from, but love him too much to leave him there. Because of the unique route by which each camper comes to Christ, it is possible you will run into questions or barriers or confusion and not know how to respond. Remember Jesus is with you, not against you; send up a prayer for clarity. There are illustrations that may be helpful. For example, the word "believe" in our culture doesn't fully convey what John 3:16 means by "everyone who believes in him." The tightrope walker Charles Blondin gave us a good illustration in 1859 when he walked a tightrope across Niagara Falls. The crowds responded enthusiastically when he asked if they believed he could walk across with a man on his back, but when he pointed out a man at the front of the crowd and said, "You sir, climb on!" the man refused. To believe is more than accepting that Jesus lived and died and rose again; to believe is to put your full weight on him alone.

When you tell a camper about Jesus, you are relating the Gospel, but it is also good to refer directly to your Bible to give authority to your words. Where should you read? Here is a selection of verses you can apply to specific situations:

Prophecy:

- Isa 53:1-6—Jesus will take the punishment for our sin

Stories about Jesus:

- Luke 2—The Christmas story
- Matt 8:23-27—Jesus calming the storm, and his disciples' question, who is this?
- John 19:16-30—Jesus' crucifixion
- Matt 28:1-10—Jesus' resurrection

Teachings of Jesus:

- Matt 11:28-30—Come to me, you who are weary and burdened
- Matt 16:24-26—Deny yourself to be my disciple
- Luke 6:27-31—Love your enemies, treat people as you want to be treated
- John 3:16-17—God so loved the world
- John 5:24—Those who believe cross over from death to life

Parables of Jesus:
- Matt 18:10-14—God cares about lost sheep
- Matt 13:44-46—Sell all to gain hidden treasure
- Luke 10:25-37—The Good Samaritan
- John 10—Jesus the Good Shepherd

Stories of the Early Church:
- Acts 2:36-41—Peter's sermon: repent and be baptized
- Acts 16:22-34—The faith of the Philippian jailer

Teachings about Salvation:
- Rom 3:21-24—A righteousness through faith
- Rom 5:6-8—Christ died for us while we were still sinners
- Rom 8:1-2—No condemnation for those who are in Jesus
- Rom 10:9-10—Faith in our heart expressed in words
- 1 Cor 15:1-8—Summary of the Gospel
- 1 Peter 2:23-25—Jesus bore our sins
- 1 John 1:5-2:2—God is light; confessing sin
- Rev 21:1-5—Heaven; God will wipe every tear from our eyes

An important way of communicating the Gospel is through your testimony, the account of how your story merged with the continuing story of Jesus. Your testimony will include your life up to the time of your initial encounter with Jesus, an account of who he is and how you put your faith in him, and a description of the changes in your life between then and now.

Paul gave a great example of this in front of King Agrippa in Acts 26. Be careful not to glorify sin by dwelling too much on your past, and keep the details appropriate to the age of your campers. When you tell your story, take your time with the middle part: how you came to faith in Jesus. Explain this key part of your story in enough detail that the camper will be able to follow your example. Some of you may have difficulty describing the changes since you became a believer, especially if you became one at an early age. Timothy also went to church in diapers, grew up as a good boy, earned all of his Sunday school pins and thought he was doing all the right things. Is that your story? Then it can be just as effective as Timothy's account. There are many campers who are growing up just as you did and yet have not realized their need for personal faith in Christ. Focus on the changes that God is bringing about in you day by day, and the things he is teaching you.

If you know ahead of time you will be telling your story, pray and get other staff to pray for you. Share from your heart (not paper) and don't be too concerned if it doesn't come out just the way you expected. God knows what your campers need to hear. Offer campers the opportunity to respond with comments or questions when you are done. Sometimes campers will want to share their life stories too, which can lead to great discussions and times of encouragement.

Some campers who are already believers will want to reaffirm their faith in Jesus, or repent from a sinful lifestyle, or recommit themselves to walking with God or serving him. In many cases, they are personalizing a faith they "inherited" from their parents, and perhaps this is the first time they understand the Gospel for themselves. This kind of conversation is not very different from what we just discussed; in fact, you should not assume a camper is already a believer because they go to church and prayed a prayer when they were very young. Talk with them about turning from sin and turning to God through faith in Jesus. Discipleship is a lifelong process, and often an experience like this at camp is a turning point in their journey. Prayerfully make the most of any opportunity to respond to a camper whose heart has become open to God. Take seriously a camper's sensitivity to sin in their lives, even if you think it is not that bad; encourage a camper who hears the call of God to service, even if you think they are too young.

When a camper has come to a spiritual decision or commitment, bring the subject up frequently throughout the rest of the week. If you don't, you might give them the impression this was just a one-time thing and now it is life as always. Help them tell people at camp about their new faith or commitment: their cabin, your supervisor, the camp speaker and others who will be excited and encouraged to hear what God has done. You have only this one-week window of time to take the camper from where they are and help them become more like Christ; others will pick up from where you leave off, but until then use your time well. Teach them about prayer, get them started in their Bible (The Gospel of Mark is simple and concise), discuss how to talk with family and friends about their decision, talk about what it is like to follow Jesus in daily decisions and lifestyle, and about how to confess things to God when they mess up. Most of all, set them an example in every aspect of life as a believer. They should see you reading your Bible, hear you pray, watch you respond to life's situations and receive your apology when you mess up. Take up Paul's challenge I have already quoted twice, "Follow my example as I follow the example of Christ" (1 Cor 11:1).

This summer you will have a small but significant part in your campers' discipleship process. Have you considered ways of extending your role in their lives? Remember the parable of the Good Samaritan we discussed earlier in relation to hurt campers: he not only helped his neighbor but also left him with a caregiver and promised to check up on him. This is a great model for your role in the life of any camper. Take on the responsibility of connecting them to a caring fellowship of believers back home, and use what means you have to reconnect with them personally. Your part in the discipleship of a camper is more than a one-week commitment; in fact, I challenge you to make it a commitment for at least one year.

Your camp may have a program or system in place to help you with "follow-up" of your campers: birthday cards you fill out while you are still at camp and that are mailed for you; a camper report or profile to record spiritual decisions; help with connecting your campers to local churches; discipleship materials sent to campers or available online; weekend retreats through the year; events, promotions, reunions or clubs that take place in the campers' communities.

Camps will do what they can afford in terms of time and money, but most find camper follow-up to be one of the most challenging parts of their ministry. Really, they are dependent on the interest and initiative of their cabin leaders to take action. There is no one in the world who can accomplish what a cabin leader can do in the life of a camper by staying in touch. It may seem a small thing to you, but it means much more to a camper. Often, by the grace of God, your contact comes just at the time she needs the encouragement or challenge. Your faithful prayers may affect the course of her life. Show you care—in Jesus' name—over the long haul.

Your first concern is for campers who are in need of a **church community** in their own town. How will you know? You need to ask them; make this one of the essential conversations of your week of camp. Some campers will already have adequate church connections; others are not yet at a place in their journey toward Christ where they will want this. Focus on the ones who have shown progress in their discipleship but are not regularly attending a church that will support and encourage their spiritual growth. A child or youth is most likely to go to a church or its youth programs because he has a personal connection with someone there. If that person is not you, the best thing you can do is to help him find a personal connection in a church near his home. Perhaps another staff member lives in the camper's neighborhood and can get him started at his church. Maybe through conversation, you will discover that a camper's grandparent or uncle is a believer. Pray that God will open doors for your campers to be included in a caring community through the year. If that is not possible, perhaps because parents are opposed to their attending, then you may be their only spiritual caregiver for the year.

Faithful prayer for your campers will make a difference you can hardly imagine and that you may not perceive until heaven. Will you commit to praying for at least one of your campers every day through the year? Write one name for each day on your calendar or as an alert on your cell phone. Ask your campers for ways you can pray for them. If you have people in your life who are prayer warriors, ask them to pray for your campers as well. Pray not only for the circumstances in your campers' lives but also for their spiritual progress, and let them know you are still tracking with them. You can see this practice in the introductions of most of Paul's letters to the churches: "We always thank God for all of you and continually mention you in our prayers. We remember before our God and Father your work produced by faith, your labor prompted by love, and your endurance inspired by hope in our Lord Jesus Christ" (1 Thes 1:2-3).

There are so many ways to **communicate** with your campers. Do you remember when people used to *talk* on their phones? It's still possible! If you call a camper at their home, be sure to identify yourself to whoever answers and explain why you are calling; if there is any resistance, thank them and politely end the call. Younger campers will not have much experience on the phone, so ask specific questions and keep it short. If you want to use Skype or another type of video call, it is best to get the permission of the parents first, even with the oldest campers.

Remember that parents may be suspicious of any adult who shows an interest in their son or daughter, and it is worth the extra effort to have that connection with them as well. This type of communication should be only occasional; some cabin leaders get enthusiastic about this idea to the point of harassment, and that is not appreciated. Texting is unlikely to contain serious conversation, but you could invite campers to text you when they need prayer or help.

Some **social media** sites require kids to be a certain age before they become members (e.g., 13 years for Facebook, Instagram and Snapchat; no limit for Twitter), so that will (or should) limit its use. However, social media raises other issues related to your online image in comparison to your camp image. Do they line up? Or will campers quickly discover a side of you (or your friends) you would rather they didn't see? Please clean up your social media before you go to camp, including Facebook, YouTube and Instagram! Crank up your privacy settings so campers will not see what friends of your friends are doing. If you need to, hide stuff—or they will find it. That said, social media can be a good way to stay in touch and follow your campers' stories, especially if you live a long way from them. But avoid trivia and shallowness; make your interactions with campers as personal and significant as they were in the cabin. Be careful not to make promises you can't keep. Consistency between your time with them at camp and online is key.

Still, nothing online has the effect of a **letter by mail**. Remember those? When is the last time you received a personal letter in the mail? Exactly! So when you send one to your camper, you have done a rather extraordinary thing. Tweets disappear in seconds and your status update is way down the newsfeed by the end of the day, but a camper might keep a letter on her bulletin board or in her Bible for years. Is it too much to write (by hand, no less!) letters to all your campers? Send them postcards then, or at least a Christmas card! You can help yourself in the summer with letter-writing resources for the winter— all week, take notes on things your campers did or said, or their interests or spiritual commitments. You could also get your campers to write a letter to themselves in the summer and send it to them in the winter, along with your own note. The fact you took the time to send them something in the mail will keep you remembered, along with all you are about.

Do you live close enough to **get together** with your campers? Again, make sure you contact and get permission from parents. "My mom says I can go" is not enough; you should take responsibility to communicate and build relationships with the families. Always get together with several campers, or a camper and his friends—never one-on-one. You could grab fast food together, or go to her volleyball game. And of course, you could invite your campers who have no church to go with you to yours. If you have a place that is big enough (and if you are brave enough), you could even invite the whole cabin for an overnighter. I have known parents who have driven a long way to make something like this happen. Be sure the parents understand that you—not the camp—are responsible for this event. Make pizzas or cookies together, look at camp photo albums or videos, relive the fun of camp and spend some time talking about your life with Jesus.

Are you excited about what God will do through you this summer? My prayer is you will enter the temporary community of camp with confidence in God's gifting and the humility to let him do what only he can do. May you be bold in prayer and gentle with the Gospel, and filled with a love that welcomes campers for who they are and refuses to leave them there. I hope you will decide to track with your campers' discipleship for a minimum of one year.

If this book has been helpful to you and you have seen God answer my prayer, I would be happy to hear about it. You can write to me at:

- Email: jimbadke@gmail.com
- Facebook: facebook.com/jimbadke
- Blog: jimbadke.blogspot.com.

God go with you, to camp!

Post Amazing God Experience
Syndrome (P.A.G.E.S.)

Sometimes coming home from a Christian camp at the end of a week or summer is like stepping out from under an umbrella into the pouring rain. You feel bombarded by many things that you were mostly protected from at camp: sensual TV commercials; people with selfish attitudes and foul mouths; lurid temptations you had practically forgotten about. Suddenly the prayers of your supporters are less, the anxieties of life are greater, and the world presses in on you with all its weight.

The first weeks after camp are a dangerous time for camp staff, and more than one has quickly fallen for some trick of the devil, the lure of the world or a re-kindled desire of the heart, causing more damage than the good that was accomplished by their ministry. Even those who stand strong may miss the intensity of the camp community so much that it is

125

hard to stay motivated in the mundane sameness of life at home. It is like pulling yourself out of the best book you ever read to find that even the colors in your room look dull in comparison.

May I suggest that the sooner you turn the page after your amazing God experience at camp, the better you will adjust to the next adventure he has for you. The camp experience is meant to be temporary; the view from that mountaintop was designed to help you find your way better when you got back down. God called you to camp, but it was so he could send you back into the world better equipped to fulfill his purposes there. Jesus sent his disciples into the world with this prayer: "My prayer is not that you take them out of the world but that you protect them from the evil one. They are not of the world, even as I am not of it. Sanctify them by the truth; your word is truth. As you sent me into the world, I have sent them into the world" (John 17:15-18).

Ask your prayer supporters to keep remembering you during this time. Maintain the spiritual disciplines that carried you into and through your camp experience. But most of all, get quickly re-connected with the church. If you are regularly involved and serving at your camp but not at a local church, there is something wrong. The church has a right to benefit from the experience and training you gain at camp because it is the Body of Christ, God's chosen instrument to bring the Gospel to the world and build up believers.

Here is Paul's advice to young Timothy: "Don't let anyone look down on you because you are young, but set an example for the believers in speech, in life, in love, in faith and in purity" (1 Tim 4:12). Maybe you really want to work with junior high youth as you did at camp, or operate the sound system or play in the worship team as you know you are able. Maybe your church is watching to see how well you change diapers in the nursery first.

Whether it is the nursery or kids club or mowing the church lawn, do it so well and with such drive and commitment that they can't miss your example. People need nurseries. Change diapers and burp babies with a servant's heart, as Jesus would. Set them an example in your daily life and morality as well. Don't give them one reason to look down on you simply because of your age. Jesus said that those who are faithful in a few things will be entrusted with more (Matt 25:21). Believe him!

Christian Camping Associations and Ministries

- Christian Camping International (World): cciworldwide.org
- Christian Camping International (Canada): cci-canada.org
- Christian Camp and Conference Association (USA): ccca.org
- Global Outreach: globaloutreachgroup.org
- Children's Camps International: childrenscampsinternational.com
- Youth for Christ Camps: yfc.net/camp
- Young Life Camps: younglife.ca
- Intervarsity Christian Fellowship Canada: Camps: ivcf.ca

Secular Camping Associations

- International Camping Fellowship: campingfellowship.org
- Canadian Camping Association: ccamping.org
- American Camp Association: acacamps.org

Camp Search

- Our Kids: ourkids.net
- Kids' Camps: kidscamps.com
- My Summer Camps: mysummercamps.com
- Summer Camps: summercamps.com
- Camp Page: camppage.com

Camping/Youth Ministry Resources

- Youth Specialties:
  youthspecialties.com
- YouthMin:
  youthmin.org
- Youth Leader Stash:
  youthleaderstash.com
- Download Youth Ministry:
  downloadyouthministry.com
- Simply Youth Ministry:
  youthministry.com
- Ultimate Camp Resource:
  ultimatecampresource.com
- YouthWorker:
  youthworker.com
- Center for Youth/Parent Understanding:
  cpyu.org
- Camp Games:
  campgames.org
- EGAD Ideas:
  egadideas.com
- Christian Camp Pro:
  christiancamppro.com

Made in the USA
Lexington, KY
15 June 2018